OUC Business English 101

商大生のための
ビジネス英語101

国立大学法人小樽商科大学創立100周年記念
ビジネス英語プロジェクトチーム編著
小樽商科大学出版会

Preface

　小樽商科大学（OUC: Otaru University of Commerce）は、2011年7月に創立100周年を迎えました。この百年間に、実業界を中心に、実にさまざまな分野に多くの卒業生が進出し、輝かしい成果と社会への貢献を果たしてきたことは自明です。小樽商科大学は、実学、語学、品格をモットーに、ゼミナールを何よりも重視し、少数精鋭の教育を一貫として参りました。中でも、英語教育は、商大の柱のひとつであり、実業界でも英語教育界においても高い英語力を駆使して日々活躍している逸材を輩出するのに大きな貢献をしてきたものと自負しております。

　この度、本学創立100周年を記念して、本書「商大生のためのビジネス英語101」が小樽商科大学出版会（OUC Press）から刊行されることとなりました。本書はその名の通り、商大でのビジネス英語関連の授業で使用されることを意図としています。101はアメリカの大学の科目コードで使用される「初級」または「基礎」を意味し、本書はビジネス英語初心者を対象にした内容と構成になっております。

　商大生にとって、ビジネス英語とは何か。また、大学生にとってもビジネス英語とは何であるのか。そもそもビジネス英語とは何であろうかという疑問も起きると思います。21世紀のビジネスシーンは、旧来の商業英語などに見られる貿易関連の文書の作成という限定的なものではありません。また、近年までテレビやラジオの英会話で取り上げられていた、オフィスシーンや電話会話などの話し言葉だけの枠を超えた、マルチな機能を含むものへと変貌しております。その代表的なものがインターネットの爆発的普及に伴う英文情報の入手機会、および電子メールによる個人間の英文でのインターラクションの機会の増大です。さらに、人前で特定のテーマについて効果的なスライドを駆使したプレゼンテーション力が営業に携わるビジネスパーソンだけでなく、技術者にも求められる時代になっております。

　こうしたビジネスシーンのパラダイムシフトが起きている現在に於いて、ビジネスの実務経験がない大学生がビジネス英語を学ぶ意義について考える必要があります。オフィスの英会話やビジネス交渉の実務的なインターラクションをロールプレイしても果たしてどれほどの意義があるものかと考える方もいらっしゃるでしょう。会話主体の授業にビジネスシーンのスキットを多少入れればビジネス英語の授業になるのでしょうか。それは、現在のビジネス英語の実態のほんの一

部を扱ったものでしかありません。また、教室内での社員と顧客との電話の英会話は英語力そのものの強化にはまことにけっこうな効果的なタスクであるかも知れませんが、それはあくまでも将来の使用場面の設定でしかありません。

　まだ就職していない、また企業研修も受けていない大学生でもあっても、実はビジネスの世界にはすでに深く関わっています。それはまず、顧客として生まれてから今日まで買い物やアパートの賃貸契約を始めとする商業活動に関わっているという事実です。また、アルバイトなどを通して接客などの実務をすでに体験している大学生もいるでしょう。すなわち、ビジネスシーンの基本的構成要素である財とサービスの提供側とそれを受ける側である顧客のうち、後者の側に既にいるのです。要は、前者の側に立つ準備の時期と内容の問題です。

　前者の財とサービスの提供側である企業人、または今日的にはビジネスパーソンに必要な英語力は、就職後の企業内研修で培われると考え、大学ではビジネス英語に特化した内容のシラバスやカリキュラムは不要と考える方もいらっしゃるかも知れません。しかし、それは日本の大学全体の雰囲気そのものであり、北の精鋭である小樽商科大学では事情は異なります。我らは商科大学であり、ビジネスに特化した内容で英語を教えることに躊躇する必要は微塵もありません。また、金融界、メーカー、サービスなどさまざまな分野に卒業生が就職する中で、皆が皆英語を必要としているわけではないと言う方もいます。それでは、皆が皆必要としている大学の科目などは現実にあるのでしょうか。

　就職した段階で新入社員の英語力によって配属が決まる企業も少なくありません。すなわち、大学の4年間に培われた英語力で勝負が決まるのです。しかし、即戦力として使える英語力とはオフィス英会話が自由自在にできるものというわけではありません。オフィスで使う英語程度は、しっかりとした英語の実力が備わっていれば速習できます。結論として、オフィスでの場面を想定して学習する時間が将来あるのであれば、英語の基礎力を盤石なものとすることが先決です。ビジネス用語を覚えるより、まず一般的な日常会話やメールでの使用頻度の高い語彙をまず身に付けるべきです。いわゆるESP (English for Specific Purpose) よりもEGP (English for General Purposes) を優先しなければなりません。

　では、大学生のための初級ビジネス英語の何を学べばよいのでしょうか。それは、いま現在、在学生としての立場にある現実を学習の対象とすることです。顧客としての立場には既にあるということは確認しましたが、ビジネスパーソンの側の視点はどうなるのでしょうか。そこで、本書では、現役の大学生が財とサー

ビスの提供側の場面のセッティングとして、第1に実務に関わる前に企業のケースやビジネスに関係する英語文献を通じた研究と発表、第2に英語を使ったアルバイトでの接客（service encounter）、第3に将来のキャリアの決定、外資系企業や社内会話を英語にするなど就職後英語を使用する可能性が高い企業への問い合わせや英文履歴書や英語の就職面接を含む就職活動（job hunting）の3つを「大学生のためのビジネス英語初級の必要事項」と位置づけ、さまざまなタスクを通じて英語を学び、それを強化し、ビジネス関連の知識も同時に増やしてもらうことが期待されています。

　本書は、初級とうたっていますが大学の何年生でも使用できる内容となっています。就活はまだ先と考えている新入生もアルバイトを始める人もいるでしょう。すでに自分を売り込み、企業活動に関与する時期にいる人もいるでしょう。また、本書は本学のe-learningシステムとも連動しており、本文中の対話文の音声やタスクの解答なども確認できるようになっております。本書を通じて、伝統ある我が商大のさらなる100年に向けて、強力な英語力を駆使して世界に羽ばたいていただければ幸いです。

　北に一星あり　小なれど　その輝き強し

執　筆　者

国立大学法人小樽商科大学創立100周年記念ビジネス英語プロジェクトチーム

　小林　敏彦　小樽商科大学大学院商学研究科アントレレナーシップ専攻教授
　Shawn M. Clankie　小樽商科大学言語センター教授
　大島　稔　小樽商科大学言語センター教授
　Ibrahim Farouck　小樽商科大学言語センター助教
　マイケル・T・金子　小樽商科大学大学院商学研究科現代商学専攻院生

TABLE OF CONTENTS

Preface ——————————————————————————————— 01

CHAPTER I. Getting Started

    UNIT 1: Talking About Your Dream Job (1)
        STEP 1: Planning Your Future ——————————————— 11
        STEP 2: Talking about Your Future ——————————— 13
        STEP 3: Understanding Corporate Structures ———— 14
        STEP 4: Listening for Comprehension ——————————— 17
        STEP 5: Listening for Perception ——————————————— 18
        STEP 6: Discussion ———————————————————————— 19

    UNIT 2: Talking About Your Dream Job (2)
        STEP 1: Listening for Comprehension ——————————— 20
        STEP 2: Listening for Perception ——————————————— 21
        STEP 3: Grammar ———————————————————————— 22
        STEP 4: Proper Questions & Responses ————————— 25

    UNIT 3: Describing Companies
        STEP 1: Learning Conversational Phrases ———————— 27
        STEP 2: Substitution Drill ——————————————————— 28
        STEP 3: Expansion Drill ———————————————————— 29
        STEP 4: Comparing Two Companies —————————— 30
        STEP 5: Discussion ———————————————————————— 31
        STEP 6: Reading a Business Case ——————————————— 32
        STEP 7: Vocabulary Review ———————————————— 45

CHAPTER II. Job Hunting

UNIT 1: Classified Ads
STEP 1: Useful Words & Phrases ———————————————— **49**
STEP 2: Reading Classified Ads (Reading) ————————— **50**
STEP 3: Vocabulary Check ——————————————————— **51**
STEP 4: Questions ——————————————————————— **51**
STEP 5: Writing an E-mail (1) ————————————————— **51**
STEP 6: An Example E-mail ——————————————————— **52**
STEP 7: Making a Phone Call (1) ———————————————— **53**

UNIT 2: CV
STEP 1: How to Write a CV in English ——————————— **55**
STEP 2: Reading an E-mail (1) ————————————————— **60**
STEP 3: Vocabulary Check ——————————————————— **60**
STEP 4: Questions ——————————————————————— **60**
STEP 5: Writing a CV —————————————————————— **61**
STEP 6: An Example CV ————————————————————— **62**
STEP 7: Making a Phone Call (2) ———————————————— **63**

UNIT 3: Job Interview
STEP 1: Useful Words & Phrases ———————————————— **64**
STEP 2: Reading an E-mail (2) ————————————————— **65**
STEP 3: Vocabulary Check ——————————————————— **65**
STEP 4: Questions ——————————————————————— **65**
STEP 5: Writing an E-mail (2) ————————————————— **66**
STEP 6: Writing an E-mail (3) ————————————————— **67**
STEP 7: Having an Interview —————————————————— **68**

UNIT 4: Common Q & A for Job Interviews
- STEP 1: Greetings at a Job Interview —————————————— 71
- STEP 2: Why You Want to Work for the Company ——————— 72
- STEP 3: What You Know about the Position and the Company —— 73
- STEP 4: What You Can Do for the Company ———————————— 74
- STEP 5: Asking Your Background ————————————————— 75
- STEP 6: Asking Your Expertise ————————————————— 76
- STEP 7: Job Preferences ————————————————————— 77
- STEP 8: Your Career Goals ————————————————————— 78

CHAPTER III. Service Encounters

UNIT 1: Working at a Souvenir Shop
- STEP 1: Serving Customers ————————————————————— 81
- STEP 2: Substitution Drill ——————————————————— 82
- STEP 3: Explaining about Products ————————————————— 83
- STEP 4: Dealing with Problems ——————————————————— 84
- STEP 5: When Trouble Happens ——————————————————— 85
- STEP 6: What's Wrong with the Signs? ————————————— 89

UNIT 2: Working at a Restaurant
- STEP 1: Fast Food Restaurant ——————————————————— 91
- STEP 2: Sushi Restaurant ————————————————————— 92
- STEP 3: Taking an Order at a Japanese Food Restaurant ———— 93
- STEP 4: Making Menus & Notices ——————————————————— 94
- STEP 5: Listening to a Recipe ——————————————————— 96
- STEP 6: Cooking Vocabulary ————————————————————— 97

UNIT 3: Expressing Whatever You Want
  STEP 1: Communication Strategies ———————————— **98**
  STEP 2: Word Matching ——————————————————— **100**
  STEP 3: Creative Framework ————————————————— **101**
  STEP 4: Guess What I Mean ————————————————— **103**
  STEP 5: Express Yourself ——————————————————— **105**

CHAPTER IV. Presentation

UNIT 1: What is a Presentation?
  STEP 1: Understanding Presentations ——————————— **107**
  STEP 2: The Difference between Classroom Presentations and Business
    Presentations ———————————————————————— **108**
  STEP 3: Common Mistakes Made by Students in Classroom Presentations
  ———————————————————————————————— **109**
  STEP 4: Tips for Successful Business Presentations ——————— **110**

UNIT 2: Outlining a Successful Presentation
  STEP 1: Deciding Your Subject ———————————————— **111**
  STEP 2: Using Additional Information for Support —————— **115**
  STEP 3: Sample Presentation ————————————————— **117**
  STEP 4: Tips for Using PowerPoint —————————————— **118**

CHAPTER V. Discussion

UNIT 1: Japanese & American Ways of Discussion
    STEP 1: Differences in Japanese and American Discussion Styles (1) —— 121
    STEP 2: Differences in Japanese and American Discussion Styles (2) —— 122

UNIT 2: Practice Discussion
    STEP 1: Sample Discussion Dialogue 1 —— 123
    STEP 2: Sample Discussion Dialogue 2 —— 125
    STEP 3: Discussion —— 126
    STEP 4: Tips for a Group Discussion, Meeting, Conference, or Forum —— 127
    STEP 5: Extra Practice —— 128

Appendix

Appendix 1: Getting to Know Each Other —— 135
Appendix 2: Useful Dialogs for Business Persons —— 136
Appendix 3: Describing OUC —— 141
Appendix 4: 交通機関の標識 (A) —— 143
Appendix 5: 交通機関の標識 (B) —— 145

CHAPTER I

Getting Started

UNIT 1: Talking About Your Dream Job (1)

STEP 1: Planning Your Future

みなさんは自分自身の人生について、どのような未来像を頭に描いていますか。ちょっとここで整理してみましょう。まず以下の質問に自分自身について答えて、選択肢のアルファベットを○で囲んでください。

1. What are you going to do after you graduate from college?
    A. Get a job.
    B. Go on to graduate school.
    C. Others: _____
    D. I'm undecided. / I don't know.

2. What career are you seeking? What is your **dream job**?　〔第一希望の職〕
    A. I would like to be a(an) _____.
    B. I'm undecided. / I don't know.

3. Do you have a part-time job now? If so, what?
    A. _____.
    B. I don't have a part-time job now.

4. Would you like to continue your current part-time job as your future career?
    A. Yes, because _____.
    B. No, because _____.
    C. I'm not sure.

5. What should you consider in deciding your occupation? Indicate the importance of each item in the scale by choosing one of the five: 1. not important / 2. not very important / 3. neither important nor unimportant / 4. important / 5. very important. Then, arrange them in the order of importance. Put a number in each bank.

[__] aptitude & taste（適性・好み）	1	2	3	4	5
[__] location of workplace（勤務地）	1	2	3	4	5
[__] salary / wages（給与・賃金）	1	2	3	4	5
[__] self-achievement（自己達成）	1	2	3	4	5
[__] social status & honor（社会的地位・名誉）	1	2	3	4	5
[__] stability（安定性）	1	2	3	4	5
[__] working conditions（労働条件）	1	2	3	4	5

6. What would you like to achieve in the future? What is your dream?
    A. I would like to _____.
    B. I don't know.
    C. I have no dream.

7. What are your strengths and weaknesses?

Strengths	_____ _____ _____
Weaknesses	_____ _____ _____

CHAPTER I: Getting Started

STEP 2: Talking about Your Future

以下のダイアローグを参考にして、将来の職業、希望就職先や業種、さらに、将来達成したい夢について自由に英語で話し合ってください。また、囲まれたフレーズとほぼ同じ意味を表すフレーズを下から選んで吹き出しに書き入れてください。

> Don't mention it. / What would you like to be most? / Could you tell me? / It must be interesting. / I really don't know. / I appreciate it. / What a wonderful idea!

A: What is your dream job? [1]
B: Dream job? That's a good question. I really don't know what I want to be, but I have a dream.
A: Dream? Let me hear it. [2]
B: Sure. I want to travel around the world.
A: You mean on business?
B: Not necessarily. I want to sail around the globe.
A: How?
B: Many ship companies offer services to travel around the world, stopping by several ports, taking several months or years.
A: Sounds interesting. [3] But do you think you have enough time to do so while having a job?
B: That's a really good question. I'm not sure. [4] Maybe I should be a sailor or become rich enough to travel after retirement.
A: Or maybe you can telework, traveling around the globe while using the Internet.
B: That's a wonderful idea! [5] I didn't think of that. Thank you so much! [6]
A: You're welcome. [7]
B: Now let me hear your dream job.
A: Sure.

STEP 3: Understanding Corporate Structures

　民間企業にはさまざまな業種があり、さらにそれぞれの企業の中では通常は、分業化・階層化され、営業、経理、人事などの特定の役割を担当する部門が組織化されています。自分の就職先を決める場合は、どの業種かだけでなく、どの部門で働くかも考慮すべきでしょう。財務会計をしたい人は、どこの会社に入っても自衛隊に入隊しても財務会計の仕事があります。ここでは、企業の一般的な構造と役職をタスクを通じて学びます。

TASK 1: 左側にある企業内の主要部門を表す和文に一致する英文を線で結んでください。

和文：

和文	英文
[1] 経理・財務	accounting & finance
[2] 研究開発	communications
[3] 広報	general affairs
[4] 市場開発	marketing
[5] 事業	operations
[6] 総務	personnel (HR: human resources)
[7] 人事	public relations
[8] 通信	R&D
[9] 販売	sales

TASK 2: 企業の業種と企業内部門の一覧表を参考に、以下の質問に自問自答するかペアまたはグループで話し合ってください。

1)　What kind of company would you like to work for? Why?
　　_____

2)　Which department are you interested in working at? Why?
　　_____

企業の業種と企業内部門一覧表
Check your choice / preference.

	finance & insurance	government offices	information & communications	manufacturing	services	wholesalers & retailers	others
accounting & finance							
communications							
general affairs							
marketing							
operations							
personnel (HR)							
public relations							
R&D							
sales							

Task 3: Seeking Your Career

以下は、過去の小樽商科大学 (OUC: Otaru University of Commerce)の就職先の業種ランキングです。それぞれの業種に対してあなたが将来選択する可能性はどのくらいありますか、A, B, C, D, Eの中から選んで○で囲んでください。また、このランキングについてどう思うか、ペアワークで話し合ってください。

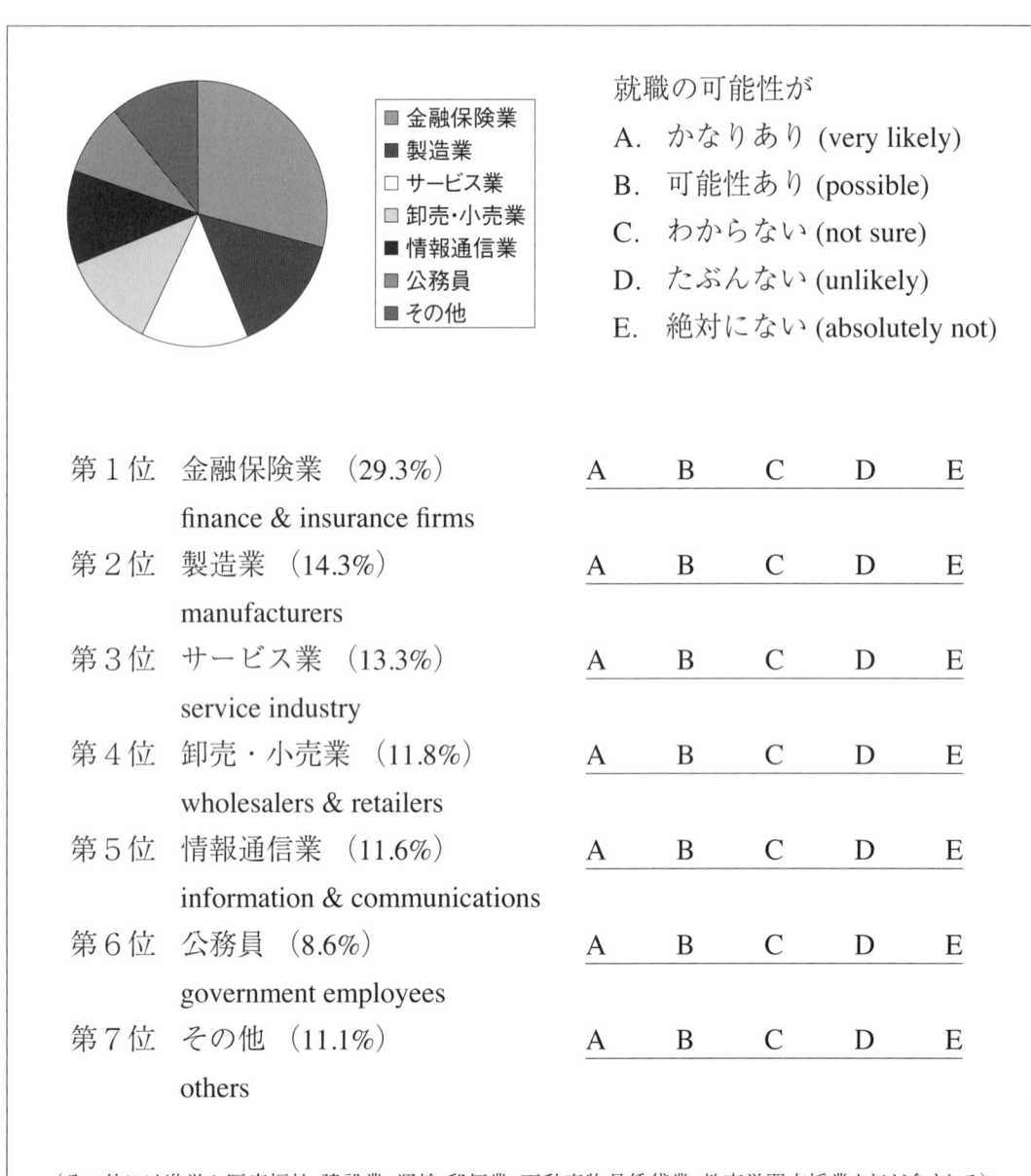

就職の可能性が
A. かなりあり (very likely)
B. 可能性あり (possible)
C. わからない (not sure)
D. たぶんない (unlikely)
E. 絶対にない (absolutely not)

		A	B	C	D	E
第1位	金融保険業 （29.3%） finance & insurance firms	A	B	C	D	E
第2位	製造業 （14.3%） manufacturers	A	B	C	D	E
第3位	サービス業 （13.3%） service industry	A	B	C	D	E
第4位	卸売・小売業 （11.8%） wholesalers & retailers	A	B	C	D	E
第5位	情報通信業 （11.6%） information & communications	A	B	C	D	E
第6位	公務員 （8.6%） government employees	A	B	C	D	E
第7位	その他 （11.1%） others	A	B	C	D	E

（その他には進学や医療福祉、建設業、運輸・郵便業、不動産物品賃貸業、教育学習支援業などが含まれる）

CHAPTER I: Getting Started

STEP 4: Listening for Comprehension

OUC e-learning 音声ファイルにアクセスして音声を聞いてください。

二人のビジネスマンが小樽運河 (Otaru Canal)付近で初めて会ったときの会話を聞いて、聞き取れた情報と憶測 (guesswork)に基づいて、下記の図表の適所に書き入れてください。言及のない項目については、x を書き入れてください。

		The First Speaker	**The Second Speaker**
1.	NAME		
2.	COMPANY		
3.	DUTIES & POSITION		
4.	BUSINESS SITUATION		
5.	WHERE THEY LIVE		
6.	HOBBIES		
7.	PERSONALITY		
8.	AGE		
9.	NATIONALITY		
10.	ACADEMIC DEGREE	bachelor's / master's / doctor	bachelor's / master's / doctor
11.	MARITAL STATUS	single / married	single / married

その他聞き取った対話の内容をメモしよう。

STEP 5: Listening for Perception

OUC e-learning 音声ファイルにアクセスして音声を聞いてください。
もう一度、対話文を聞いて聞き取った語句を書き入れるか、語句を選択してください。

A: Hello, my name is Hosoki Kenta from (**1. an / the / φ**) Hanya International. Nice to meet you.

B: Hello, my name is Michael Kaneko. I run (**2. an / the / φ**) souvenir shop at Otaru Canal. Nice to meet you too.

A: How's business?

B: Very slow. The number of tourists coming to Otaru has been (**3. decreasing / increasing**) gradually. 〔客足がない時に使うフレーズ〕

A: Oh, really? How do you (**4. _____**) it?

B: We need to keep presenting something new to our customers so they won't (**5. _____**) bored with our goods and services. What are your (**6. _____**) ?

A: My company is a small trading company mainly importing from Korea and China. Our business is slow too, so we need to (**7. expand / extend**) our business to other areas of Asia.

B: Sounds like you have a lot of (**8. responsibility / responsibilities**).

A: Yes, indeed. Where do you import your goods from?

B: Most of them are domestically made, but some are imported from China and Taiwan.

A: I see. Then we can be business partners, (**9. _____**) we?

B: Yes, let's sit down there and talk.

A: Sorry, but I have to leave now. I have to catch a plane at 3:30 at Chitose. Can I have your business card? Here is mine.

B: Sure. Here it is. Is this your email address? 〔何かを手渡す時のきまり文句〕

A: Yes. Let's keep in touch. I come to Otaru every month. 〔別れても連絡を取り合いたいとき使える〕

B: Sounds great. Nice (**10. _____**) you, Mr. Hosoki.

A: Nice (**10. _____**) you too, Mr. Kaneko.

B: Have a safe trip. 〔旅行へ出る人にかける決まり文句〕

A: Thank you. Good luck with your business. 〔相手に何かの成功を祈る時には、Good luck with ___. のパターンが使える〕

B: Thank you. You too.

A: Thanks.

STEP 6: Discussion

　対話文の内容について以下のそれぞれの英文の内容に同意するか同意しないか、5段階にスケールに印を付けてから、モデルダイアローグを参考に、その理由や根拠についてペアワークで話し合ってください。

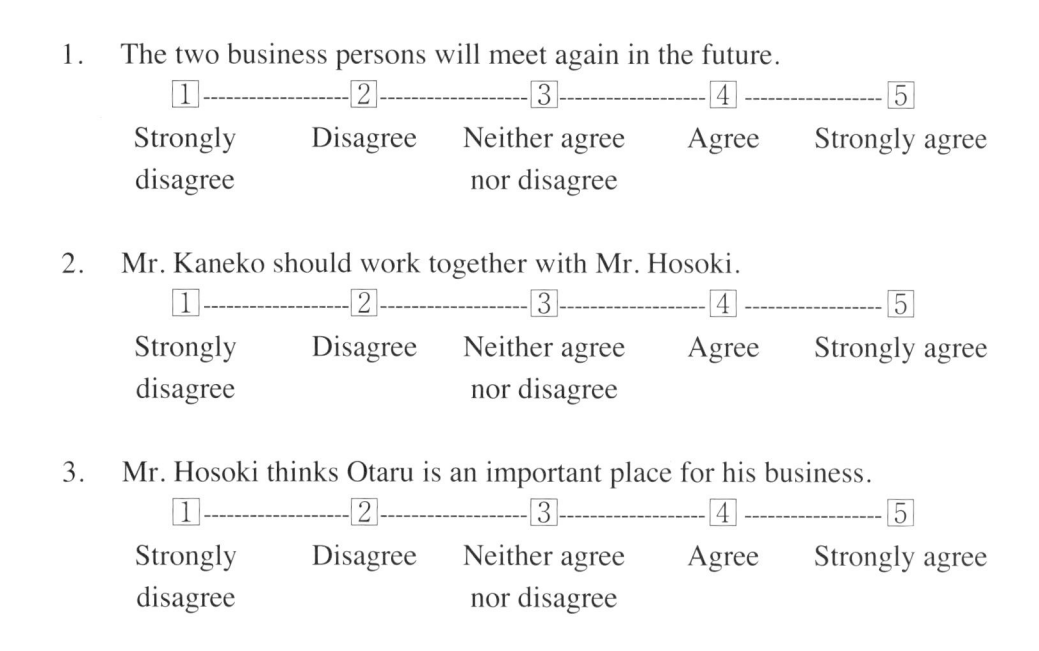

1. The two business persons will meet again in the future.

    ①――――②――――③――――④――――⑤
    Strongly   Disagree   Neither agree   Agree   Strongly agree
    disagree   nor disagree

2. Mr. Kaneko should work together with Mr. Hosoki.

    ①――――②――――③――――④――――⑤
    Strongly   Disagree   Neither agree   Agree   Strongly agree
    disagree   nor disagree

3. Mr. Hosoki thinks Otaru is an important place for his business.

    ①――――②――――③――――④――――⑤
    Strongly   Disagree   Neither agree   Agree   Strongly agree
    disagree   nor disagree

MODEL DIALOG

A: Hi, I'm Taro. Nice to meet you.
B: Hi, I'm Yoshiko. Nice to meet you too.
A: Do you think the two men will meet again?
B: Yes, I think so.
A: Why do you think so?
B: Mr. Hosoki said, "Then we can be business partners, can't we?" This shows he was willing to meet Mr. Kaneko again.
A: Yes, but when Mr. Kaneko told him to sit down and talk, he flatly refused that offer.
B: That's because he had a plane to catch.
A: Do you think it was true? I doubt it.
B: I disagree. I think he was telling the truth. He suggested exchanging business cards. He really wanted to talk to Kaneko more but he had to leave.
A: Well, he said that simply because he felt somehow guilty rejecting the offer.

UNIT 2: Talking About Your Dream Job (2)

STEP 1: Listening for Comprehension

OUC e-learning　音声ファイルにアクセスして音声を聞いてください。

　細木さんと金子さんが学生時代の思い出と将来の事業について話し合っています。聞き取った情報を以下の表の適切な個所に英語または日本語で書き入れてください。

	Mr. Hosoki	**Mr. Kaneko**
学生時代の部活動 college day club activities		
学生時代のバイト college day part-time work		
仕事上の問題 problems on business		
今後の事業展開 future business operations		

STEP 2: Listening for Perception

OUC e-learning　音声ファイルにアクセスして音声を聞いてください。
もう一度細木さんと金子さんのダイアローグを聞いて、聞き取った冠詞を選択してください。

Kaneko: Mr. Hosoki, how was your college life? Did you belong to any club or circle?

Hosoki: Yes, I belonged to (**1. a / an / the /φ**) English communication circle. How about you?

Kaneko: I didn't belong to any because I was busy with my part-time jobs.

Hosoki: What did you do?

Kaneko: I did many jobs. One of the main jobs was working at (**2. a / an / the /φ**) souvenir shop. I worked for (**3. a / an / the /φ**) Marine Kan for four years.

Hosoki: Four years? That's why you now run (**5. a / an / the /φ**) souvenir shop.

Kaneko: That's right. I found it quite interesting to serve tourists and talk to them. I learned how to explain about (**6. a / an / the /φ**) products and other things well. Why did you belong to (**7. a / an / the /φ**) English circle?

Hosoki: I really wanted to improve my English skills not just for (**8. a / an / the /φ**) fun but for my future career. I've wanted to work globally since I was (**9. a / an / the /φ**) child. I understood English is absolutely essential to make my dream come true.

Kaneko: And you've made it!

Hosoki: Yeah.

Kaneko: Good for you.

Hosoki: Thank you.

Kaneko: What is your goal or target of your business?

Hosoki: To tell you the truth, I'm quitting my company to start my own business.

Kaneko: Oh, really? What are you going to start?

Hosoki: I'm planning to focus on (**10. a / an / the /φ**) trading some particular goods and services like (**11. a / an / the /φ**) glasswork or metal work. How about you, Mr. Kaneko?

Kaneko: I really want to increase (**12. a / an / the /φ**) number of outlets and open shops in other places like Sapporo and Chitose.

Hosoki: Sounds great. I hope you can make it.

Kaneko: Thank you.

STEP 3: Grammar
英語の冠詞の使い方を整理しよう

　何年英語を勉強しても冠詞 (article)の使い方がよく理解できないという人が多くいます。理解できていると思っていても、いざ話したり書いたりするときに迷ったり、間違った使い方をしてしまう人も多いでしょう。しかし、以下にある規則をしっかりと理解するだけで頭の中ですっきりと整理できるでしょう。英文を読む時に冠詞の有無や使い方に今後はよく注意してみましょう。また、冠詞は英語をたくさん書いて添削を受けることでより確かな使える知識となります。

名詞の前の冠詞の有無

a/an	限定されない単数の可算名詞	I have a picture.
the	限定される単数の可算名詞	I have the picture.
	限定される複数の可算名詞	I have the pictures.
	限定される不可算名詞	You can have the love you need to live.
φ	限定されない不可算名詞	I can have security.

可算名詞 (countable noun)
鉛筆や本など具体的な形があり、ひとつ、ふたつ（一本、二本、一冊、二冊）と数えられる物体や具体的な事項。

不可算名詞 (uncountable noun)
概念や思想などの抽象名詞 (abstract noun)や、そのままでは独立した形としては数えられない水などの物質名詞 (material noun)。

限定されない・限定されるとは？

限定されない	限定される
新情報 初めて提示されるもの	旧情報 前に一度出てきたもの
A: I have **a** picture. B: What kind of picture?	A: I bought this picture yesterday. B: I like **the** picture.
非共有情報 何を指しているかよくわからない	共有情報 何を指しているかはっきりわかる
A: Open **a** door. B: Which door?	A: Open **the** door. B: Okay.
抽象的情報 意味が抽象的	具体的な情報 意味が具体的
A: Why do you like this place? B: Because I can have security.	A: What kind of love can I have? B: You can have **the** love you need to live.

限定詞
(determiner)
名詞句の前に付いてその名詞の概念が該当する範囲を限定する語

<u>冠詞</u>	a / an / the
<u>数量詞</u>	some (-) / any (-) / every (-) / each / no (-)
<u>指示形容詞</u>	this / that
<u>代名詞の所有格</u>	my / our / your / his / her / their

限定詞は一緒に並ばない。
(x) Some my friends speak French.
→ Some of my friends speak French.
→ Some friends of mine speak French.

限定詞は疑問詞の前には置かれない。
(x) Tell me the what you like.
→ Tell me what you like.

以下は英字新聞のリードの部分です。適切なものを選択してください。

Brain-dead man's family OK's organ donations

Kyodo News

The family of (**1: a / the / φ**) man who was declared (**2: a / the / φ**) brain dead has given its approval for his organs to be donated, although he never expressed his wishes in writing, marking (**3: a / the / φ**) first such case under (**4: a / the / φ**) revised Organ Transplant Law, (**5: a / the / φ**) transplant organization said Monday.

(The Daily Yomiuri, Tuesday, August 10, 2010, p.1)

Child abuse cases mark record high

181 police investigations in Jan.-June

(**1: A / The / φ**) police investigated 181 cases of (**2: a / the / φ**) alleged child abuse involving (**3: a / the / φ**) 187 victims in (**4: a / the / φ**) first half of this year, both of which are (**5: a / the / φ**) highest figures in 2000, (**6: a / the / φ**) National Police Agency said Thursday.

(The Daily Yomiuri, Friday, August 6, 2010, p.1)

CHAPTER I: Getting Started

STEP 4: Proper Questions & Responses

OUC e-learning　音声ファイルにアクセスして音声を聞いてください。

音声を聞いて、それぞれの質問に対してもっとも自然で適切な返答を選んでください。

1. _____
    A. Nice to meet you.
    B. Nice meet you too.
    C. Nice meeting you.
    D. Nice meeting you too.

2. _____
    A. How do you do?.
    B. I'm fine.
    C. Why?
    D. No problem.

3. _____
    A. To improve my listening skill.
    B. Because I was not informed of it.
    C. I'm fine, thank you.
    D. I have three classes today.

4. _____
    A. Nobody knows.
    B. No, I don't.
    C. I just remembered.
    D. It may be difficult.

5. _____
    A. The day before yesterday.
    B. Shizuoka.
    C. Five hours.
    D. By train.

6. _____

    A. I'm glad.
    B. I work for a city government.
    C. For world peace.
    D. I have no idea.

7. _____

    A. I work every day.
    B. I'm an architect.
    C. I usually watch TV.
    D. Mostly.

8. _____

    A. I'm a CFO.
    B. On the 7th floor.
    C. It depends.
    D. It is very competitive.

9. _____

    A. I'd like to ask you something.
    B. I'm moving out of town.
    C. I'd like to go on to graduate school.
    D. I'm a Buddhist.

10. _____

    A. No problem.
    B. Why not?
    C. See you.
    D. Maybe.

UNIT 3: Describing Companies

STEP 1: Learning Conversational Phrases

OUC e-learning 音声ファイルにアクセスして音声を聞いてください。

音声を聞きながら以下のダイアローグのスクリプトを読んで重要フレーズの使い方を理解してから、先生の指示に従ってそれぞれのフレーズを使った置き換えドリルと拡張ドリルをしてください。

A: Excuse me. You must be Mr. Hosoki? I'm Michael. Do you recognize me?
   (久しぶりに会った人に自分のことを覚えているか確認する決まり文句)

B: Yes, of course. We met at Otaru Canal, didn't we?

A: Yes. How have you been? *(How are you?よりも久しぶり会った感じが出る。)*

B: Fine. I'm sorry, I didn't respond to your mail at all.

A: That's okay. How's business? *(ビジネスの調子や景気を聞くときに使われる決まり文句)*

B: Not very good. We had some problems with our clients in Hong Kong and I had to fly over again and again.

A: That sounds really hard for you. Have you solved the problems? *(何かたいへん苦労している人を労う時に使えるフレーズ)*

B: Almost.

A: You came to Otaru on business this time?

B: No. I came to attend my alumni party.

A: College?

B: Yes.

A: Are you by chance an OUC graduate? *(by chance を付けることで、「もしかして」というニュアンスが出せます。)*

B: Yes.

A: What a coincidence! Me, too. *(何かの偶然に驚いた時に使うフレーズ)*

B: Oh, really? When did you graduate?

A: In 1984. How about you?

B: In 1988. You graduated the year I entered college.

A: So, we just missed each other. *(どこかの場所や時点で入れ替わりとなり、接点がなかった時に使える決まり文句)*

B: Right. Do you have time now?

A: Sure. Let's sit and talk.

STEP 2: Substitution Drill （置き換えドリル）

空欄を入れ替えてセンテンス全体を復唱しましょう。

---

1. **Do you recognize _____?**　～に見覚えがありますか。

    ⇒ this restaurant
    ⇒ this man
    ⇒ this bag
    ⇒ that photo
    ⇒ that car

---

2. **We had some problems with _____.**　～と問題が生じました。

    ⇒ our customers
    ⇒ our clients
    ⇒ our partners
    ⇒ our users
    ⇒ our subcontractors

---

3. **Are you by chance _____?**　ひょっとしてあなたは～でしたか。

    ⇒ an architect
    ⇒ a realtor
    ⇒ a bank clerk
    ⇒ a government worker
    ⇒ a tennis player

CHAPTER I: Getting Started

STEP 3: Expansion Drill（拡張ドリル）

下線部を付け足してセンテンス全体を復唱しましょう。

---

1. **Do you recognize _____?** 〜に見覚えがありますか。

    ⇒ this restaurant
    ⇒ this restaurant under the railway
    ⇒ this restaurant under the railway that was crowded
    ⇒ this restaurant under the railway that was crowded with students

---

2. **We had some problems with _____.** 〜と問題が生じました。

    ⇒ our customers
    ⇒ our customers in China
    ⇒ our customers in China who were not satisfied
    ⇒ our customers in China who were not satisfied with our service

---

3. **Are you by chance _____?** ひょっとしてあなたは〜でしたか。

    ⇒ the architect
    ⇒ the architect who designed the monument
    ⇒ the architect who designed the monument in the park
    ⇒ the architect who designed the monument in the park near the airport

STEP 4: Comparing Two Companies

2つの企業の概要(overview)をよく見て、それぞれの項目に該当する英語を以下から選んで所定の空欄に書き入れてください。次にそれに続く質問をペアワークで聞き合ってください。

business activities / capital / company address / company name / date founded / net income / number of employees / operating income / president and representative director / sales / starting salaries / total assets

_____ (商号)	**Hanya International**	**Billiken Shop Michael**
_____ 代表取締役社長	Hosoki Kenta	Michael Kaneko
_____ 創立（創業、設立）	June 28, 1965	April 1, 1984
_____ 資本金	200,000,000 yen	3,000,000 yen
_____ 事業内容	international trading	souvenir sales
_____ 所在地	Suidobashi, Chiyoda Ward, Tokyo	Irifune, Otaru, Hokkaido
_____ 従業員数	780 (200)	1 (2)
_____ 初任給（月給）	250,000 yen	Unknown
_____ 売上高（昨年）	280 million yen	12 million yen
_____ 総資産	1.2 billion yen	75 million yen
_____ 営業利益	120 million yen	0.5 million yen
_____ 純利益	55 million yen	0.3 million yen

CHAPTER I: Getting Started

STEP 5: Discussion

Q1. Which of the two companies would you like to work for? Why?
_____

Q2. What do you like and dislike about each company? Write down your likes and dislikes about each in the tables below.

Hanya International

LIKES	
DISLIKES	

Billiken Shop Michael

LIKES	
DISLIKES	

31

STEP 6: Reading Business Cases

　ビジネスケース（以下、「ケース」と呼称する）とは、特定の企業の過去から現在の様子を記述したものです。さまざまな業種の企業が日本語や英語を始め、多くの言語で書かれています。さまざまな業種のケースが本学の大学院商学研究科アントレレナーシップ専攻（OBS: Otaru Business School）を始めとする世界中のビジネススクールでテキストとして使用されています。ここでは、語学出版社の語研の英文ケースを取り上げます。よく読んで以下の質問に簡潔に答えてください。また、下線部の用語の意味をよく確認しながら読み進めてください。

Q1: Q&A
以下の質問に簡潔に英語または日本語で答えなさい。
What kind of company is Goken?

Q2: Multiple-Choice
以下の質問の答えとしてもっとも適切なものを選んでください。
What is the current situation surrounding foreign language textbook publishers like?
　A. Hopeful.
　B. Saturated.
　C. Slow.
　D. Hopeless.

Q3: True or False
本文の内容に一致しているものにはT，一致していない、または言及のないものにはFを選んでください。
　1) Goken has been publishing books mainly for business persons.　　(T / F)
　2) Goken plans to make their lineup more multilingual.　　(T / F)
　3) Goken is threaten by the diversified language resources from other media.
　　　　　　　　　　　　　　　　　　　　　　　　　　　　　　　(T / F)
　4) Goken has clear strategies to compete with their competitors.　　(T / F)
　5) Goken finds it necessary to shift their focus to target new customers.
　　　　　　　　　　　　　　　　　　　　　　　　　　　　　　　(T / F)
　6) The book market is relatively easy for anyone with the know-how of developing books to enter.　　(T / F)

A Case of Goken: Product Development and Marketing in the Overflooded English Textbook Market

Author(s) Kobayashi, Toshihiko

Citation 小樽商科大学人文研究 (2007), 114: 21-36

Issue Date 2007-09-30

URL http://hdl.handle.net/10252/223

ABSTRACT

> 概要：全体の要点をまとめた部分です。

The fever for learning English shows no sign of cooling down in Japan. The vast space allotted for English **self-learning** books is **over-flooded** with English conversation and preparation materials for **TOEIC** tests. In the era of low sales of books, the publication industry has been joined by up-and-coming **publishers** who **saturate** the market with similar products with very similar book titles. Publishers can be categorized as **manufacturers** just like food and industrial makers. However, they have attracted almost no attention as a subject for **case study**. What is the book market really like and what marketing strategies has each publisher worked out to develop new products and promote their sales? Goken, which has long enjoyed its status as a producer of **quality** books for learning a wide range of foreign languages has a typical size as a publisher in Japan and is thus suitable for study. Descriptions in this case are largely based on the information, knowledge and opinions gained from Mr.Okumura Tamio, Goken's department manager, in a series of interviews through face-to-face interactions and e-mail exchanges. First, a brief description of Goken will be made and an attempt will be made to uncover the current situation surrounding foreign language textbook publishers. Second, the features of Goken's **materials development** and **marketing strategies** will be analyzed.

1. A Brief Description of Goken

The Goken **Co, Ltd**. is located in Sarugaku-cho, Chiyoda Ward, Tokyo. The company was **established** in February, 1963 with **capital** of 15 million yen. The publisher specializes in self-learning materials such as books, cassette tapes, CDs and sound files, for a wide range of languages spoken in 22 countries and regions in the world including English, French, German, Italian, Spanish, Portuguese, Russian, Dutch, Arabic, Persian, Chinese (Mandarin), Cantonese, Taiwanese, Korean, Vietnamese, Thai, Filipino, Malay, Indonesian, and Japanese.

As of January, 2007, Goken has a total of 13 **employees** (5 in the editorial, 4 in sales, and 4 in general and financial sections) and Mr. Tanaka Minoru (born in November 4, 1958) is the president, who assumed the position on March 20, 2003. In August, 1976, the company established Today Book, a **subsidiary company**, to develop materials. In 1980, Goken started to publish materials for languages other than English. In 1999, the publisher's total annual number of books sold reached 120,000 copies. In 2006, the total number of the book titles reached 500. In 2006 alone, Goken published 27 new titles and **reprinted** 37 **existing** titles. Goken's **annual sales** for 2005 reached 315 million yen. Among the 9246 publishers and related businesses in Japan, Goken comes in the 2771st in sales (Teikoku Data Bank).

2. The Real Picture of Publishers in Japan

The Japanese publishing industry has been suffering from a long **structural recession** due to low sales of books and magazines. People are becoming busier and have difficulty sparing time for reading. They can also get information and knowledge from other resources, such as TV and the Internet, quickly and more importantly, less costly. People are **getting tighter with their money** for the traditional charged resources of information.

One **poll** conducted by Nihon Ryutsu Sangyo Shinbum (2006) reports the average amount of money an individual in Japan spends for books is 2,628 yen a month. Japanese have **been straying from** printed letters and words. People are reading fewer books and this trend is particularly true of the younger generation. Besides, with a lot of large bookstores and used bookstores such as Book Off opening **outlets** in cities, a number of medium and small-sized bookstores have been forced **out of business**.

CHAPTER I: Getting Started

2-1. Diversified access to information and knowledge

Now we can read newspapers on the Internet. This relatively easy access to information has led to a decline in sales of **hardcopy** papers in many countries in the world. Nevertheless, this trend is not seen yet in Japan, where people traditionally prefer to read papers delivered to their homes early in the morning and/or in the evening.

Newspapers are not the only media that are available without charge. Many major magazines, articles, radio, TV and other media now provide free web contents that are almost equivalent to the hard cover versions. Moreover, sound files recording narrations of news scripts are now freely obtained from **archives** such as those of **VOA (Voice of America)**. With scripts and sound files, learners of foreign languages can now get almost equal or even more materials from such free resources to/than regular textbooks sold in stores.

Goken does not see the **diversification** of language resources from other media as a direct threat to their publication business. While having some concerns about such free resources, Goken still believes in the superiority of **hardcopies**. Books are portable with no need for electricity or any bulky devices and are more friendly on the eyes than computer or other electronic monitors.

2-2. The ceaseless Japanese fever for learning English

In Japan, there has been a publication rush of English self-learning materials (hereinafter referred to as "English textbooks"), primarily on English conversational phrasal books and TOEIC preparation kits. Statistics released by Shuppan Kagaku Kenkyujo based on figures collected between January and October in 2006 show a total of approximately 70,000 new titles were published, of which 930 titles were on learning foreign languages. Moreover, 500 titles were English textbooks. This means roughly 1.7 English textbooks were published daily during that period. On top of this, best sellers and popular existing titles were reprinted. In reality, however, most of the titles ended up with the initial print and then go out of print.

Enthusiasm for learning English is likely to continue in Japan. Many businesses now oblige their employees to take the TOEIC test periodically for **placement** and/or other purposes. In 2002, **the Ministry of Education, Science, Culture and Sports** compiled a strategic project to nurture Japanese who can use English as a specific action plan in an

35

attempt to make drastic improvements in English teaching for Japanese. This strategic plan was proposed in response to our social awareness that is essential for children to acquire communicative skills in English to survive in the 21st century amid economic and social **globalization**, and this is becoming a very important issue in light of children's futures and our nation's further development. Under this action plan, the English **proficiency** levels required of all Japanese nationals were suggested in specific ways. By the time they graduate from junior high school, students should be able to be engaged in greetings and elementary level conversation in English (again along with the same level of reading, writing and listening required). By the time of graduating from high school, students should be able to talk about daily topics in English (along with the same level of reading, writing, and listening required). More specifically, average junior high school students should be able to pass the **STEP 3rd grade**; and high school students should be able to pass the 2nd grade by the time they graduate; college and university students should be able to pass the STEP pre-1st grade, get 550 in **TOEFL**, and/or get 730 in TOEIC before they graduate.

In response to this policy, several attempts have been made including the introduction of a listening comprehension test as part of **the Center Examination** in 2006; the designation of 100 high schools "Super English Language High Schools" for **state-of-art** English teaching and research; promoting full-time employment of foreign nationals; providing more scholarship offered to high school and college students wishing to study abroad through exchange programs. English is also about to be taught formally as a required subject in elementary schools.

As used as one of the criteria for the target proficiency for students to reach, the Eiken or the STEP (Society for Testing English Proficiency) seemed to attract more **applicants**. In reality, however, the number of STEP applicants has been decreasing due partly to the declining children's population from the low birth rate and partly due to the Ministry of Education, Science, Culture and Technology's abolishment of **the approval system** for almost all quality exams in Japan. The Eiken used to call itself the "Mombusho-approved STEP." There has been a gradual fall in the number of STEP applicants in the recent figures:2,536,666 in 2003; 2,492,287 in 2004; 2,484,414 in 2005. Likewise, the TOEFL (Test of English as a Foreign Language) has been losing popularity since the switch from paper-based to computer-based administration and subsequent major changes in test

CHAPTER I: Getting Started

contents. With the declined popularity, many publishers have stopped developing materials for the STEP and TOEFL tests.

2-3. The Saturated English textbook market

In large bookstores, a large display space is allotted for language learning books, primarily English textbooks, which can be divided into three broad types: English conversation, listening practice and test preparation kits. Books for English conversation typically introduce words and phrases with pages organized and displayed according to the situation, and/or notion/function. Listening books are designed primarily for comprehending news in English using authentic resources mostly from the radio or web sites. Test preparation kits are for those taking TOEIC, TOEFL or STEP tests. Recently, English grammar books, especially for speaking are getting more popular.

The English learning book market **is nearly saturated with** materials of a variety of titles, genres, content, volumes, cover designs, layouts, prices and authors. In each of the properties above, publishers are **racking their brains** to make their materials distinct from other publishers and attractive to gain readers. However, since popular genres among learners that lead to good sales are now clearly identified and focused on, publishers tend to target them and develop books with very similar or almost identical titles, such as those starting with "Native", or with similar contents and prices.

Because of the flood of books with similar titles and contents, both shop clerks, who should be able to give some advice to customers about what to read for their purposes, and customers are rather confused and have difficulty finding materials that fulfill their needs. Thus, both are easily allured by tempting titles or subtitles or cover designs that do not necessarily reflect the quality of the contents.

Publishers needs to have capable editors who are familiar with the know-how of developing books and competent marketing staff who grasp the "pre-modern or outdated publication distribution system" (Mr. Okumura) to enter the market. In the book development process, however, technological advancement in editing with personal computers has allowed editors to do at their own desks what used to be done by **printers**, which has shortened the whole publication process as well as reduced costs for book development. Beside, no large machines or facilities are needed for the work. Therefore, as far as book development is concerned, the book market is relatively easy for anyone with the know-how of developing books to enter. Yet, there is much more concern in marketing their products in the pre-modern or outdated system.

2-4. Price competition

In terms of price competition, there is a wide range of prices of books that publishers **arbitrarily** set. Publishers specializing in technical books with a relatively small **readership** tend to have high prices and can coexist without much concern about competition from other publishers by creating separate market niches. They can focus on their favorite genres that are often disregarded by others. On the other hand, publishers of competitive areas such as English textbooks are required to check out the prices that other publishers set in order to launch their own **competitive prices**. Moreover, large publishers without a prior publication record of any English textbooks and non-publishers are joining the English textbook market. Newly entering companies often have contracts with some celebrities or renowned individuals from fields irrelevant to English teaching such as TV personalities or singers to write English conversation books with expectations of large sales from the authors' big names.

Besides, nowadays **prestigious** foreign textbook publishers such as Oxford and Cambridge are now developing books **tailored for** Japanese learners of English and marketing them in Japan with branch offices or subsidiaries operating in Tokyo. They try to achieve large sales with expectations from the publishers' own fame. Because of these factors, price competition has been intensifying in the textbook market with the shortened **product life cycle** and similar titles and/or contents.

2-5. TOEIC way out in front

ETS, the Educational Testing Service in Princeton, New Jersey, develops and administers both the TOEFL and the TOEIC. It announced that over 4,500,000 people take the TOEIC test throughout the world every year. In 2003, 1,423,000 people took the TOEIC test in Japan. In 2004 and 2005, the number increased to 1,433,000 and 1,495,000,respectively. The number of TOEIC **examinees** is on the rise and thus materials preparing for the test are the lead product in the English textbook market in Japan. Many businesses, colleges and universities use the test scores for **placement**, **evaluation**, **grading**, and/or replacing course credits.

An analysis indicates that there are nine profitable areas of foreign language textbooks: TOEIC preparation, English conversation, English grammar, English vocabulary, English listening, Chinese, Korean, French and Japanese. Naturally, publishers tend to focus on these clearly identified genres for more profits. Among these, TOEIC related books are the most profitable product as guaranteed by the increasing number of those who take the test voluntarily or those who are forced to take it by their companies or schools. Thus, TOEIC books occupy the largest sales floor or bookshelf space.

TOEIC had long kept the same question style until May, 2006 in Japan, when major changes were made such as narrating choices that used to be written out on the test and narrating by four speakers of different English dialects-American, Canadian, British, and Australian which used to be by American English speakers only. Moreover, selective segments, writing and speaking through computers were introduced in January, 2007. These changes have made previous test preparation kits (books and CDs) all useless and thereby an additional rush of publication is now continuing.

2-6. Proposal-oriented sales strategies

In relation between publishers and bookstores, bookstores traditionally make decisions as to what, when, where, and how to present books at their sales spaces. Publishers usually do not meddle in sales of books at stores; they merely introduce new books by sending stores regular mails or faxes or having sales representatives visit them.

Between bookstores and customers, customers select what they want with their own will, while bookstores do nothing but display books in attractive ways or at most with some promotion copies demonstrated on the wall. They just wait for customers to pick up a product and bring it to their cashiers for payment.

Currently, however, publishers are trying to get more involved in promoting sales at stores with "proposal-oriented sales strategies". Publishers can now grasp the exact number of copies of particular titles sold at stores through **the POS (Point of Sale) system** and give advice and/or suggestions directly to the bookstores as to the **lineup** and presentation in order to bring profits to both bookstores and themselves. In addition, now large publishers are launching active sales promotion campaigns through other media.

In the relationship between publishers regarded as sellers and bookstores as buyers, it is not the publishers that decide which book and how many copies to ship. It is distributors such as Tohan, Nippan, and Osakaya, that stand between publishers and bookstores. Bookstores basically receive products from **distributors** and display them to sell at their places. Books are replenished whenever they get out of stock at stores by stores ordering the titles from the distributors.

On the other hand, between bookstores seen as sellers and customers as buyers, customers cannot negotiate prices at regular books stores, which is the first **sales channel**, because book prices are supposed to be the same throughout Japan, as guaranteed by **the resale price maintenance system** that prohibits discounts of first-hand books. However, selling second-hand books at used bookstores or through net auction sites at arbitrary prices by used bookstores or auction bidders is permitted.

3. The Current Situation of Goken

Goken has published a total of 43 new titles of books on TOEIC as of January, 2007. Of the 27 titles published in 2006, nine were on TOEIC, which **accounted for** 60% of all the English textbooks. In contrast to the **dominance** of TOEIC test, the STEP and the United Nations Associations Test of English are losing popularity and Goken has no plan to publish any materials related to these two tests.

Goken names three publishers as their major **competitors**—J Research, Velet, and The Japan Times—and analyzes them briefly as follows. J Research has the 3rd largest share of the TOEIC market in Japan. The company's strongest point is their price competitiveness and sales promotion. Velet has published introductory books for a wide range of Asian and European languages. In particular, the publisher has a good reputation of their clearly explained introductory books and Goken feels threatened by their skillful promotion and advertizing. The Japan Times has a well established system to develop quality books that match the needs of learners of English by providing with a wide range of lineups covering the four language skills (listening, speaking, reading and writing).

3-1. Goken's Quality Control

Goken has a large lineup of quality books covering a variety of genres for developing English language skills. Goken has published few books with exaggerated titles such as "You can master XXXX words in XX weeks." Many of Goken's books target highly motivated intermediate and advanced level learners of English and try to facilitate learning through continued efforts on the part of learners themselves.

Goken has long used computer programs to develop learning theories to maintain their products' reliability and practicality based on **authentic** data used in the real world. In particular, **corpus linguistics**, which researches a collection of written and spoken material in machine-readable form, has played an important role in **lexical analyses** including identifying frequency of particular words and phrases to develop data-based vocabulary textbooks for **FEN**, TOEIC and TOEFL. Goken is a pioneer in such a scientific approach to lexical analyses to provide quality products. By using a corpus, they can make more objective selections of materials that reflect the real-life language use than that which were merely selected with authors' rather subjective judgment and intuition.

While the majority of publishers for language learning materials develop books for just a few popular languages such as Chinese, Korean and French, Goken has distinguished itself from other publishers in the number of languages they develop materials for. Goken has published books for as many as 22 languages. Goken takes advantage of its multilingual lineups and often uses the titles or the contents of popular English textbooks for other language textbooks, and vice verse.

3-2. Shortened product life cycle and the process of new product development

Unlike essays and novels, which rarely become outdated, language textbooks have a short **product life cycle** of 1.5 years on average (Okumura). The shortened cycle compelled to keep on and on developing and publishing new titles taking on distinct features to be competitive in the over-flooded English textbook market. Publishers tend to publish new books with relatively short intervals. Goken published 27 new titles in 2006. The product life cycle of test preparation kits generally terminates when the styles of questions change. Information and descriptions in dictionaries soon become **obsolete** due to the tremendous technological innovation and concurrent reservoir of newly-born lexical items. On the other hand, books that describe how to learn a foreign language and how famous language experts learn a language seem to have some truth that hardly become outdated. However, new learning methods can be worked out and proposed that utilize new technological devices such as the i-Pod and MP3 files. Thereby, no eternity is guaranteed.

As the product life cycle has shortened, so has the process of materials development. The way an idea for a new book is proposed and developed into a book is usually divided into two types. One is called the "in-house development project", in which editing staff work out a new idea on the basis of recent analysis of popular books or requests from learners. The other type is "author-proposed project", where authors propose their ideas directly to publishers often with some sample pages or whole manuscripts. With Goken, more than 80% of their past books have been developed by editing staffs. When a new proposal is made, they try to find an appropriate author to write the new book, sometimes by inquiring the authors they know or by contacting new authors. To contact new textbook writers, they sometimes check out the bookshelves at stores and find out who has written what and then try to get their contact information through college or university websites if they are college teachers. Goken usually prefers authors who know about Japanese learners of English and the Japanese culture and society because they believe these are the very important factors that should be definitely considered when writing books to sell in Japan. Naturally, they ask someone living in Japan. It is also the case that authors introduce other authors.

As for **royalty** agreements, Goken uses a typical range for the publishing industry. In the depressed publishing industry, publishers increasingly have come to pay royalties on the basis of the copies actually sold. And some fail to pay because of their worsened financial records. In contrast, Goken pays authors their royalties usually **in installments** on the basis of the number of copies published and without any delay or failure. Goken intends to continue this traditional payment. In general, publishers are in a position stronger than authors in the royalty agreement.

3-3. Sales promotion key to survival

Goken is fully aware that there is much room for improvement in their marketing strategies such as establishing new selling routes to **differentiate** their products from others. Goken thinks their promotion strategies are not well organized to sell what sells well and they are looking for ways to work out solutions.

At present, Goken has four staffs in charge of promotion who regularly visit bookstores throughout Japan. Goken also introduces new books on their own website (http://www.goken-net.co.jp/), run newspaper ads in The Yomiuri Shimbun and The Nikkei Shimbun several times a year, send emails irregularly to readers and bookstores who request information. Goken analyzes that their ineffective promotion is due to their failure to sell what sells well at appropriate times and places. Besides, this comes from their strong commitment to quality products. Goken is now trying to publish a new book in less than a year after an idea is proposed, but usually fails. Goken traditionally spends longer than other publishers for editing work to make more careful materials development and this often leads the publisher to miss good selling timing.

Goken's selling networks have been changing into being POS-basis, but not enough yet. As a result, it is often the case that good selling books **go out of stock** at large bookstores, while they are left unsold at smaller stores. However, publishers cannot intervene in the product distribution and cannot oversee it. Moreover, Goken finds it essential to promote the sales of their products through large-scale advertisement. In reality, however, they cannot afford to **allocate funds** in this way.

In addition, Goken is fully aware that they are behind their competitors in terms of **selling power** and price competition. Their weak selling power mainly comes from the lack of manpower for the sales section. Because of the continued **structural recession** of the publishing industry, Goken had to reduce the staff at the sales department in favor of those at the editing department, which is the essential part of the company to keep developing new books. Moreover, this reduction led to the scarcity of the sales staffs well aware of the nature of language textbooks and capable of working out strategies to promote sales for their products.

3-4. Goken's competitiveness

Price competitiveness necessarily declines unless publishers take measures to maintain their selling power. Goken gets profits of approximately 40% of the cover price of a book after developing costs for books and attached CDs, advertisements, distribution, and royalties payments to authors are deducted. This means a copy of a book, say, of 1,600 yen sells each time, they get a profit of 600 yen.

New learning methods using **state-of-art** technological devices such as the i-Pod as well as CDs and DVDs are spreading among learner. Cassette tapes or CDs used to be sold separately at much higher prices than those of the book itself. In 1990s, however, PC magazines started to attach free CDs. Some magazines started to appear for TOEIC learners that attached CDs with exercises and mock tests. As a result, many publishers began to attach a CD to a book without raising the book price, and Goken **followed suit** immediately.

More recently, some magazines started to attach free DVDs. At the moment, however, no language textbook publishers are following this practice.

Goken maintains the policy to stay away from the arena of price competition with other publishers while recognizing their lack of price competitiveness. This is because self-lightening books like language textbooks do not necessarily sell well even if their prices are low. Goken believes they can compete with other publishers as long as the prices they set for books fall within an appropriate range and the prices are seen as **reasonable** in light of their **added value**.

STEP 7: Vocabulary Review

これまで新たに学習した語句を以下に整理しましょう。

new words & phrases	Japanese equivalents	sample sentences

new words & phrases	Japanese equivalents	example sentences

CHAPTER II

Job Hunting

UNIT 1: Classified Ads

STEP 1: Useful Words & Phrases

問題に入る前に、よく使われるビジネスの用語を英語では何というか確認しましょう。

[ ] 職業: job / occupation / profession / vocation
[ ] 資格: qualifications
[ ] 職業訓練: vocational training
[ ] 労働市場: labor market
[ ] 就職活動: job-hunting / job hunt
[ ] 雇用 / 雇用者 / 被雇用者: employment / employer / employee
[ ] 労働者: worker / laborer
[ ] 従業員: employee / staff
[ ] 労働人口: work force / workforce
[ ] 労働条件: working conditions
[ ] 労働時間: working hours

STEP 2: Reading Classified Ads (Reading)

英語で書かれた求人広告をインターネットで読み、どのような内容が書かれているかを読み取りましょう。

KEG Int. Corporate Tax Technology

Position Number: 74810	Posting Date: Thursday 7 July, 2011
Location: USA- NY- New York	Education: Bachelor's degree
Position Category: Finance / Accounting	Experience: 0-1
Position Type: Full-time	Job Level: Analyst

Position Description
Corporate Tax Technology

KEG Int. Tax Technology group is responsible for managing the systems, processes, and data flows of the corporate tax department. We serve as a liaison between various groups within the tax department and between the tax department and other groups both inside and outside the firm. One of the critical functions of the group is to leverage technology tools to create process efficiencies and controls. We are also responsible for determining how changing laws and business environments impact our data flows and processes.

Candidates must be willing to assume administrative tasks in addition to comprehensive tax data and systems management. This is a great opportunity to gain practical experience in the corporate tax technology field and exposure to many areas of corporate taxation and financial reporting.

Skills Required
- Students must be eligible to work in the U.S.
- Accounting, Finance, or Computer Science majors only
- Knowledge of MS Excel and Access
- Strong communication and organization skills
- Prior corporate office experience is a strong plus, but not required
- Ability to learn in-house software and tax return preparation software
- Availability to work at least 15 hours a week.

Contact Us：Thank you for your interest in KEG Int.
For questions regarding the job, send an email to KE.GOOD.WILL@ms.com
Or phone call to 0134-27-5423

STEP 3: Vocabulary Check

本文中に出てきた以下の単語の意味を辞書を使わずに推測できていたか確認し、推測が誤っていたり、理解できない単語があった場合はチェックボックスに✓を入れてください。

[ ] bachelor's degree = the first level of college degree

[ ] liaison = someone whose job is to talk to different departments and to tell each of them about what the others are doing

[ ] firm = a company

[ ] leverage = invest or speculate money or technology on company against the strength of one's company

[ ] eligible = able or allowed to do something

STEP 4 : Questions

求人広告に関する以下の質問に対する答えを、ペアワークで話し合いましょう。

1) What kind of work is the Tax Technology Group responsible for?
2) What kind of knowledge do students need?
3) What kind of experience will be a strong plus for getting the job?

STEP 5: Writing an E-mail (1)

KEG. Int.宛てに英語でメールを作成して送りましょう。質問は、STEP1 の Questionsの内容をより具体的に問う内容のものを作成してみましょう。

From: billy-ken-no.1-turner@taiji-cow.ne.jp
To: KE.GOOD.WILL@ms.com
Subject:
Date:

STEP 6: An Example E-mail

以下にある例文を参考に、きちんとe-mailを書けていたかをチェックボックスに✓を入れながら確認してみましょう。

From: billy-ken-no.1-turner@taiji-cow.ne.jp
To: KE.GOOD.WILL@ms.com
Subject: ☐ Dear Personnel Manager of KEG International
Date: ☐ Wed, July 13, 2011 01:12:40 +0900

To whom it may concern,

Greetings.

I am writing to you today about the details of the information in the classified ad on your company's website (Ad # 34123).

The first question is about the knowledge required of the candidate. I can use MS and Excel without any problems but I don't know what exact level of ability you expect.

The second question is about "corporate office experience." I am not quite sure what you mean by that experience. Could you elaborate on that?

Thank you and I look forward to your response.
☐
Sincerely yours,
Ikeda Yoshiko

CHAPTER II: Job Hunting

STEP 7: Making a Phone Call (1)

　履歴書に記入すべき必要事項について電話で尋ねてみましょう。まずは下記のダイアログを会話がつながるように対話文を聞いて、空欄に聞き取った語句を入れて埋めてみましょう。次に、実際に声を出してペアワークしてみましょう。

OUC e-learning　音声ファイルにアクセスして音声を聞いてください。

Hello, this is Ikeda Yoshiko. I am calling about your (_____) on the Internet. May I speak to the (_____) manager, please?

Hi, Ms. Ikeda. I am the secretary of our two (_____) managers. Do you know the name of the (_____) manager you would like to talk to?

Sorry, I don't know, sir. Well, actually, today I'm calling to ask you about the (_____) of the CV, and also I would like to ask the (_____) something because I can't find the information on your website.

Oh, I see, let me connect you to Mr. Dolly Funk. He is (_____) new appointments. Hold on a second, please…

Hi, this is Funk, thank you for calling, Ms. Ikeda. I (_____) that you have some questions about the CV. How may I help you?

53

Yes, Mr. Funk. I have a question about the CV. Besides my name, address, e-mail address, cellphone number, educational and working experiences, what else should I (_____) ? Is there anything else that I should (____)?

Yes, Ms. Ikeda. If you have any awards or scores to (_____) your language skills, please write them on your CV. Are there any other questions, Ms. Ikeda?

No, that's all I need, Mr. Funk. Thank you for your great (____), sir.

(_____). Thank you for calling us, Ms. Ikeda. Have a good day. Bye.

UNIT 2: CV

STEP 1: How to Write a CV in English

　英米その他の英語圏では、日本の市販された履歴書の書式のようなものはなく、作成者が自由に何ページにも渡って書くことがある。履歴書は英語ではCV (curriculum vitae) またはresumeと言うが、前者がアメリカ英語、後者はイギリス英語であると断じている解説書があるが、それ正確ではなく、アメリカではいずれも使用され、むしろCVの方が今日では使用頻度が高い。

　履歴書をどのように書くかを考える前に、履歴書に何を書いて、何を書く必要でないかを確認する必要がある。それを決定するものは、求人条件である。履歴書の用途は、求人先に応募する際の必要書類として提出されるものである。

　応募用件に明記された項目は、最低限の情報として履歴書に記載する必要がある。求められていない情報を載せるかどうかは、本人が記載したほうが有利であるかどうか、また載せないと気が済まない、など、各自で判断すればよい。

　一般的に日本と米国の求人広告にある要件はかなり異なる。日本で当然記載されている、年齢や性別の要件は記載はしない。というより禁止されていることが多い。また顔写真を履歴書に貼って送付するような指示もない。それは年齢差別(age discrimination)、性差別(sexual discrimination)、容姿差別(discrimination based on appearance)になるからである。当然、人種、民族、宗教、国籍、身体的特徴などを要件に明記することは許されない。そのため、性別や出身地、生年月日を記載していない、氏名と住所と連絡先、学歴しか記載されていない履歴書が届く。それでも雇用する側は、それを元に拒否できず面接はする。例えば、日本では高校生や大学生がバイトでしているコンビニやファーストフード店に70歳を越えた高齢者が働いているのをよく見かける。また、米国の企業では、日本にあるような定年退職は一般的でなく、体力が続く限り本人の判断で働き続けられるところが多い。

　英語の履歴書は、何も英語圏で働いたり、英語圏の企業に応募するだけに書くわけではない。英語がビジネスの共通語となっている今、英語圏以外の、例えば中国の企業やアラブ系の企業へ就職する日本人も出てきている。その場合は、求人の要件がアメリカとは異なり、日本並に、もしくは日本よりもっと詳細な記載

をした履歴書を求めてくる可能性がある。

　また、新聞に掲載された求人広告(classified ads)に記載されているアルバイトのような業務と終身雇用 (tenured)のしっかりとしたものとでは、用意する履歴書に質的量的違いが出るのは当然である。修士号(master's degree)や博士号 (doctor's degree)を応募の要件とするような求人に対しては、詳細な業績リストや学位記などの複製も求められるだろう。

　以上のことから、英文の履歴書は、ひとつだけでなく複数用意しておく必要があるかも知れない。もっとも合理的な方法は、できるだけ詳細な英文の履歴書をひとつ作成しておき、応募要件に応じて不要な部分を削除してプリントアウトして送付するか、ファイルのままメールに添付するようにするとよいだろう。ゆえに、以下、日本で求められるレベルの詳細な履歴書の書き方を説明する。

１．氏名、生年月日、年齢、性別、国籍の書き方

　標準的な書き方として、それぞれの項目を左詰めで書いて、コロンまたスペースを置いて、または改行して記載する。

　例）氏名

　　　NAME: KOBAYASHI Toshihiko

　氏名は逆転させる必要はない。逆転させる場合でも姓はすべて大文字で表してわかるようにしよう。間違われると懸念があれば以下のように書くこともできる：

　FAMILY NAME: KOBAYASHI
　FIRST NAME: Toshihiko

　例）生年月日

　　　BIRTHDAY: June 28, 1985 / 28th June, 1985

　必ず西暦で書くように。昭和と記載したいかも知れないが通じないだろう。もちろん、曜日を書きたければ書いてもよい：

　　　BIRTHDAY: Monday, June 28, 1965

　例）年齢

　　　AGE: 26

当然であるが、数え年でなく、満何歳で書くこと。years old は書いても書かなくてもよい。

例）性別

SEX: male / female

男性ならmale、女性ならfemaleである。man / woman やboy / girl ではないので要注意。性別はSEXで表すのは一般的であるが、GENDERを使いたければそれでもかまわない。

例）国籍

NATIONALITY: Japanese

パスポートを持っている人を見ればわかるが、英語圏の書類などにNATIONALITYとあれば、JapanではなくJapaneseと国民名を書くのが一般的である。ただし、NATION OF (YOUR) NATIONALITYと書いてあれば、Japanと書き入れる。

2．現住所、連絡先等の書き方

例）住所

　　ADDRESS: 1-2-3-705 Hiragishi Toyihira-ku, Sapporo Hokkaido 062-0887 JAPAN

（郵便番号062-0887　日本国北海道札幌市豊平区平岸1-2-3-705）

日本国内の住所は、上記のようにすべて逆に記載する。マンション名などは記載しなくても、丁目、番地、部屋番号まで日本の住所を簡略する時と同じようにするとよい。郵便番号は全部大文字で書いた国名の前に置く。通り名や丁目、区などを示す時には、street / avenue / ward など英訳しないで、そのまま、X-dori / X-chome / X-ku のように表してもよい。

例）連絡先

　　PHONE NUMBER (cellphone): 080-1111-1111

　　PHONE NUMBER (home): 011-777-7777

　　PHONE NUMBER (work): 011-888-8888

　　FAX NUMBER (home): 011-777-7778

FAX NUMBER (work): 011-888-8889

E-MAIL ADDRESS (PC): toshi84123@res.otaru-uc.ac.jp

E-MAIL ADDRESS (cellphone): bakabon-happy@ezweb.ne.jp

　連絡先は、一番かけて欲しい番号または確実にかかる電話番号を筆頭に全部書く。実際に履歴書にする時に、不必要なものは削除すればよい。電子メールのアドレスも同様である。これ以外にホームページやブログ、フェイスブックなどのＵＲＬを用意しておくのもよい。

3．学歴の書き方

EDUCATION:

Graduated from Sapporo High School, March, 2004

To graduate from Otaru University of Commerce, March, 2012

　学歴も職歴も新しいものから記載し、下に行くに連れて古いものを書く。日本では一般的に卒業した高校まで記載するが、米国では最終学歴だけでよい。

　上記のように、主語を省略し、大文字で書き始め過去形で書く。大学在学中で卒業予定であれば、**To graduate from** のように不定詞を使う。そして、カンマを使って、月と年を書く。もちろん具体的な日を書いてもかまわない。

交換留学などで海外留学した経験があれば、しっかりと書くこと：

Studied at Western Michigan University as an exchange student, September, 2010 through May, 2011

また、すでに卒業していれば以下のように学位と専攻分野も明記して簡潔に書くこともできる：

Degree: Bachelor of Commerce, Otaru University of Commerce, Otaru, Hokkaido, Japan

Graduation Date: March, 2009

Major: accounting

4．職歴の書き方

Tutored two junior high school students, May, 2010 - March, 2011

Worked at Six Ten (convenience store) as a cashier, April 2008 - March, 2009

Worked at a construction site as a laborer, 2 weeks in August, 2008

大学生の場合は、バイトも立派な職歴として認められる場合もあるので、作文しておくとよい。企業名と業種と職務内容を簡潔に書くようにする。ちなみに1番上が、家庭教師、2番目がコンビニのレジ係、3番目が建設現場で肉体労働である。

5．趣味、特技、資格、その他の書き方

例）趣味

HOBBIES: table tennis / cooking / tea ceremony

QUALIFICATIONS: STEP pre-1st grade（英検準1級）/ TOEIC 870 / TOEFL ITP 565 / Accounting 2nd grade（簿記2級）

趣味（特技）は人間性を示す、大切な情報と成り得る。ひとそれぞれ異なる趣味があり、中には記載できないものもあるかも知れない。趣味でないものを書くのは虚偽記載になるが、数ある趣味のひとつを記載しなくても何の問題にはならない。常識的な判断をしよう。

6．賞罰の書き方

AWARDS AND HONORS:

3rd place in my university essay contest, December, 2011

1st place in all Hokkaido College Table-tennis Championship, November, 2010

2nd place in a local English speech contest, May, 2009

在学中にスポーツの大会や論文コンテスト、ミスコンテストなど、表彰された偉業はしっかりと書くようにしよう。その際、その大会やイベントに公式な英語名があることもあるので、主催者に確認するなどして正確に記載するようにしよう。

STEP 2: Reading an E-mail (1)

英文で書かれたE-mailを読み、どのような内容が書かれているかを読み取りましょう。

From: KE.GOOD.WILL@ms.com
To: billy-ken-no.1-turner@taiji-cow.ne.jp
Subject: About the CV
Date: Fri, 15 July 2011 08:30:20 +0900
Dear Ms. Ikeda Yoshiko Hope you are well. I am writing to you to let you know about the details of the CV You called me the day before yesterday but I may have given you the wrong information about the CV Did I tell you to write about your name, home address, cellphone number, e-mail address, education and work experiences, and awards or something? Added to these, there is one thing that you need to write on the CV That is, key skills, which means your English skills or computer skills, things of that nature. I am terribly sorry for not giving you the correct response the first time. Sincerely yours, Dolly Funk Personnel Manager, KEG Int.

STEP 3: Vocabulary Check

本文中に出てきた以下の単語の意味を辞書を使わずに推測できていたか確認し、推測が誤っていたり、理解できない単語があった場合はチェックボックスに印をつけてください。

- ☐ CV = resume
- ☐ key = most important
- ☐ terribly: very / extremely

STEP 4: Questions

E-mailに関する以下の質問に対する答えを、ペアワークで話し合いましょう。

1) Where does this message come from?
2) What is this message about?
3) What contents you should write on your CV?

STEP 5: Writing a CV

実際にKEG Int.に宛てCVをまずは自分なりに英語で作成してみましょう。

NAME:
Address:
E-mail address:
Cellphone number:
Education:
Major academic courses:
Work Experiences:
Awards:
Special Skills: **English skills:** **Computer Skills:**

STEP 6: An Example CV

実際にKEG.int.に宛てたCVを作成できていたか以下にある例文を参考に、チェックボックスに✓を入れながら確認してみましょう。

NAME: ☐ IKEDA Yoshiko
Address: ☐ 3-20-17 Midori, Otaru, Hokkaido, 047-099, Japan
E-mail address: ☐ billy-ken-no.1-turner@taiji-cow.ne.jp
Cellphone Number: ☐ 080-2011-0707
Education: ☐ Aug. 2010 – present: graduate school of Greenhill University, Japan
Major academic courses: ☐ Accounting, Finance, and Computer Science
Work Experience: ☐ 2006 – present, Nakamura Accounting Office, Hokkaido, Japan Part time assistant to the chief manager.
Awards: ☐ 2009-2010: Scholarship for Excellent Students of Greenhill University, Japan.
Special Skills: ☐ Accounting Grade II **English skills:** ☐ TOEIC 870 **Computer skills:** ☐ Practical knowledge of MS Office, Word, Excel, Power Point, ability to make webpages, weblogs, and communication by E-mail.

STEP 7: Making a Phone Call (2)

先方からかかってきた電話に対応してみましょう。まずは下記のダイアログを会話がつながるように対話文を聞いて、空欄に聞き取った語句を入れて埋めてみましょう。次に、実際に声を出してペアワークしてみましょう。

OUC e-learning　音声ファイルにアクセスして音声を聞いてください。

Hello, this is Ikeda Yoshiko. May I ask (_____), please?

Hi, Ms. Ikeda. This is Dolly Funk, the personnel manager of KEG. Int. Today I'm calling you to decide the (____) for your interview.

Hi Mr. Funk. Wow, that's wonderful, you mean, I've passed the first (_____)? Thank you so much! What should I do now?

Yes, Ms. Ikeda. I am happy to meet you soon. Before that, I need to check your schedule for your interview.

Okay, Mr. Funk. Let me check my (_____). I am available at the end of August or at the beginning of September.

Great. How about August (_____) a.m.?

(_____), Mr. Funk. I am looking forward to meeting you then. Thank you so much for calling.

The (_____) is mine. I'll see you then. Bye for now.

UNIT 3 : Job Interview

STEP 1: Useful Words & Phrases

　ここでは英語による就職面接を習います。まずは、よく使われるビジネスの用語を英語では何というか確認しましょう。

[ ] 就職面接：job interview
[ ] 面接を受ける：have a job interview
[ ] 面接をする：give a job interview
[ ] 内定をもらう：get a promise of job offering
[ ] 採用見込み数：hiring projection
[ ] 人材スカウト：head hunting
[ ] 通年採用：year-round recruitment
[ ] 有効求人倍率：job seeker-job opening ratio

STEP 2: Reading an E-mail (2)

英文で書かれたE-mailを読み、どのような内容が書かれているかを読み取りましょう。

From: KE.GOOD.WILL@ms.com
To: billy-ken-no.1-turner@taiji-cow.ne.jp
Subject: Change of the date for your interview
Date: Mon, July 18, 2011 10:20:35 +0900
Dear Ms. Ikeda Yoshiko Hope you are well. I am e-mailing you to let you know about the change of the date of the job interview. One of the candidates canceled the job-interview because of the sickness. Thus, we need to change the date of your job interview. We hope this change will not cause any problem for you but if it isn't convenient for you, please mail us. We are terribly sorry for this sudden change of the interview date. The new date is Monday, August 25, 10 a.m. Sincerely, Dolly Funk, Personnel Manager of KEG Int.

STEP 3: Vocabulary Check

本文中に出てきた以下の単語の意味を辞書を使わずに推測できていたか確認し、推測が誤っていたり、理解できない単語があった場合はチェックボックスに✓を入れてください。

    [ ] candidate: someone who is being considered for a job or is competing to be elected

    [ ] terribly: very / extremely

    [ ] convenient: useful to you because it saves your time or does not spoil your plans.

STEP4: Questions

E mail に関する以下の質問に対する答えを、ペアワークで話し合いましょう。

    1) Where does this message come from?

    2) What is this message about?

    3) Why does the change occur?

STEP 5: Writing an E-mail (2)

STEP1 のメールに対する返信文を作成してください。

From:
To: KE.GOOD.WILL@ms.com
Subject:
Date:

STEP 6: Writing an E-mail (3)

　KEG. int.に宛てたCVを作成できていたか、以下のメール例と比較してチェックしてみよう。

From: billy-ken-no.1-turner@taiji-cow.ne.jp
To: KE.GOOD.WILL@ms.com
Subject: Thank you for the e-mail
Date: Tue, July 19, 2011 08:40:26 +0900
Dear Dolly Funk, Hope you are well. Thank you for the message about the interview date. I am fine with the change. I am looking forward to seeing you at 10 a.m. , Wednesday, August 22. Sincerely, IKEDA Yoshiko

STEP 7: Having an Interview

さあいよいよ面接です！対話文を聞いて、空欄に聞き取った語句を入れて埋めてみましょう。次に、実際に声を出してペアワークしてみましょう。

OUC e-learning　音声ファイルにアクセスして音声を聞いてください。

Hello, it's a great pleasure to meet you, sir. I am IKEDA Yoshiko. (＿＿＿＿＿＿＿＿＿＿＿＿＿＿＿＿＿＿＿＿＿＿).

Hello. Nice to meet you too Ms. IKEDA. I am Dolly Funk, the personnel manager of this company. (＿＿＿＿＿＿).
First, could you please tell me why you'd like to work for us?

Yes, I am greatly interested in the accounting system because (＿＿＿＿＿＿＿＿＿＿＿＿＿＿＿＿＿＿＿＿＿＿＿＿＿＿＿＿).

I see. Well… by the way, according to your CV, you have a higher TOEIC score than other Japanese candidates from other universities. (＿＿＿＿＿＿＿＿＿＿＿＿＿＿＿＿).
And do you think your score of TOEIC guarantees your communicative ability in English?

CHAPTER II: Job Hunting

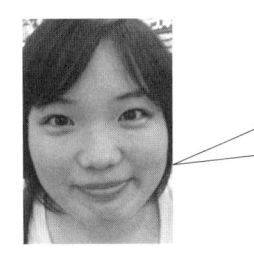

First, (_____
_____) because it is the result of small steps up every day, that is, reading a newspaper or watching NHK news programs in English and something like that. And by doing them, my communication ability is also improved I believe, but it is still not enough, though.

I see, thank you. Well, let me see, (_____
_____)?

Yes, I am writing about the brand new computer associated accounting system for companies so that they can save time on accounting. (_____
_____).

Oh, it seems to be interesting. Thank you for talking. (_____
_____). Thank you very much.

(_____).

69

UNIT 4 : Common Q & A for Job Interviews

　典型的な一連の英語面接をロールプレイします。面接で聞かれる可能性の高い質問別にステップが構成されています。それぞれの対話文の空欄の部分に自分の答えを入れてペアワークをしてみてください。なお、e-learningにアクセスすれば対話文の空欄の返答が入った完全な対話の例を聞くことができ、またスクリプトも入手できます。まずは、以下の三つの質問に対して、自問自答するかペアワークをしてください。

Warm-Up
Answer the following questions:

1) What career are you seeking? Why?
   _____

2) What would you like to be in the future? Why?
   _____

3) Which company do you want to work for? Why?
   _____

STEP 1: Greetings at a Job Interview （面接試験の始動・あいさつ）

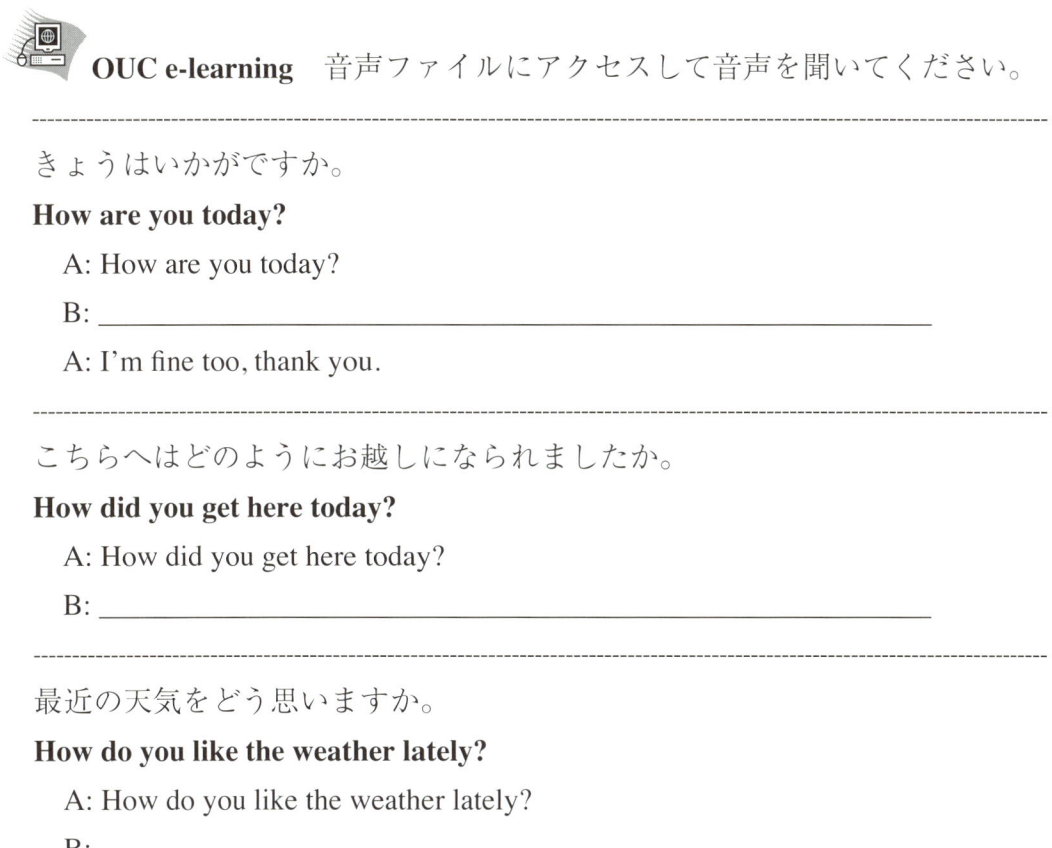

OUC e-learning　音声ファイルにアクセスして音声を聞いてください。

きょうはいかがですか。

How are you today?

    A: How are you today?

    B: _____

    A: I'm fine too, thank you.

こちらへはどのようにお越しになられましたか。

How did you get here today?

    A: How did you get here today?

    B: _____

最近の天気をどう思いますか。

How do you like the weather lately?

    A: How do you like the weather lately?

    B: _____

STEP 2: Why You Want to Work for the Company （応募の動機）

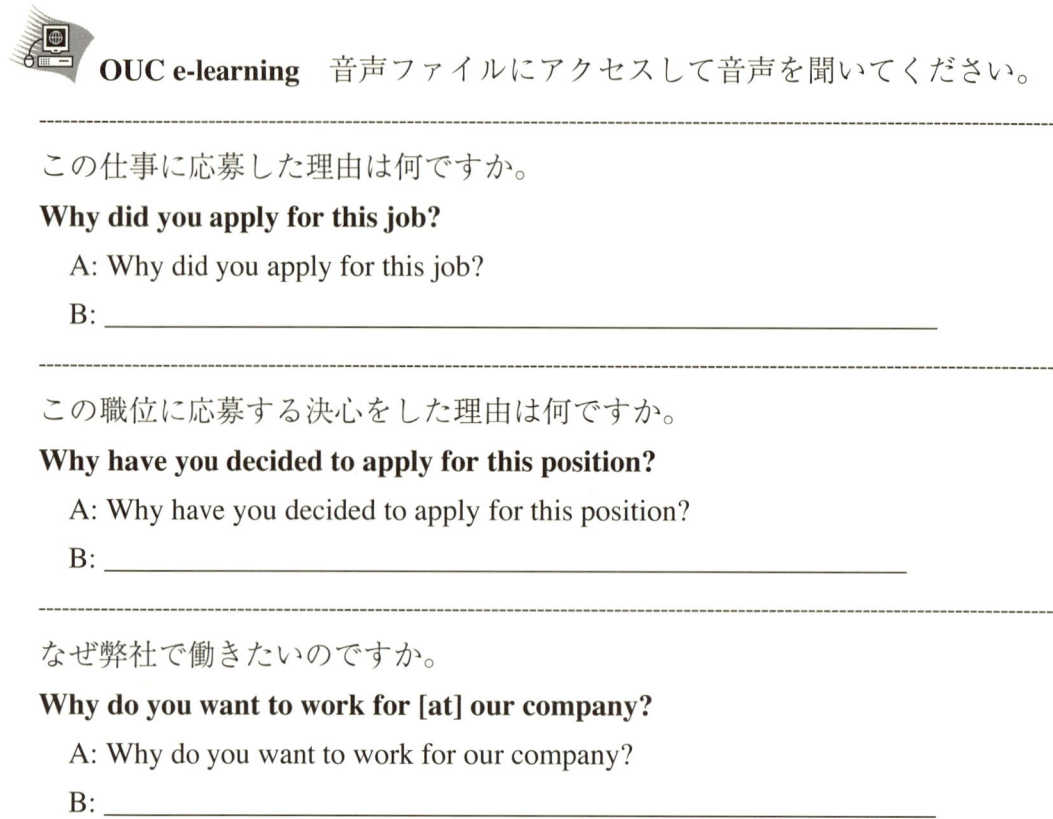

OUC e-learning　音声ファイルにアクセスして音声を聞いてください。

この仕事に応募した理由は何ですか。

Why did you apply for this job?

　　A: Why did you apply for this job?

　　B: _____

この職位に応募する決心をした理由は何ですか。

Why have you decided to apply for this position?

　　A: Why have you decided to apply for this position?

　　B: _____

なぜ弊社で働きたいのですか。

Why do you want to work for [at] our company?

　　A: Why do you want to work for our company?

　　B: _____

STEP 3: What You Know about the Position and the Company （応募先に対する知識）

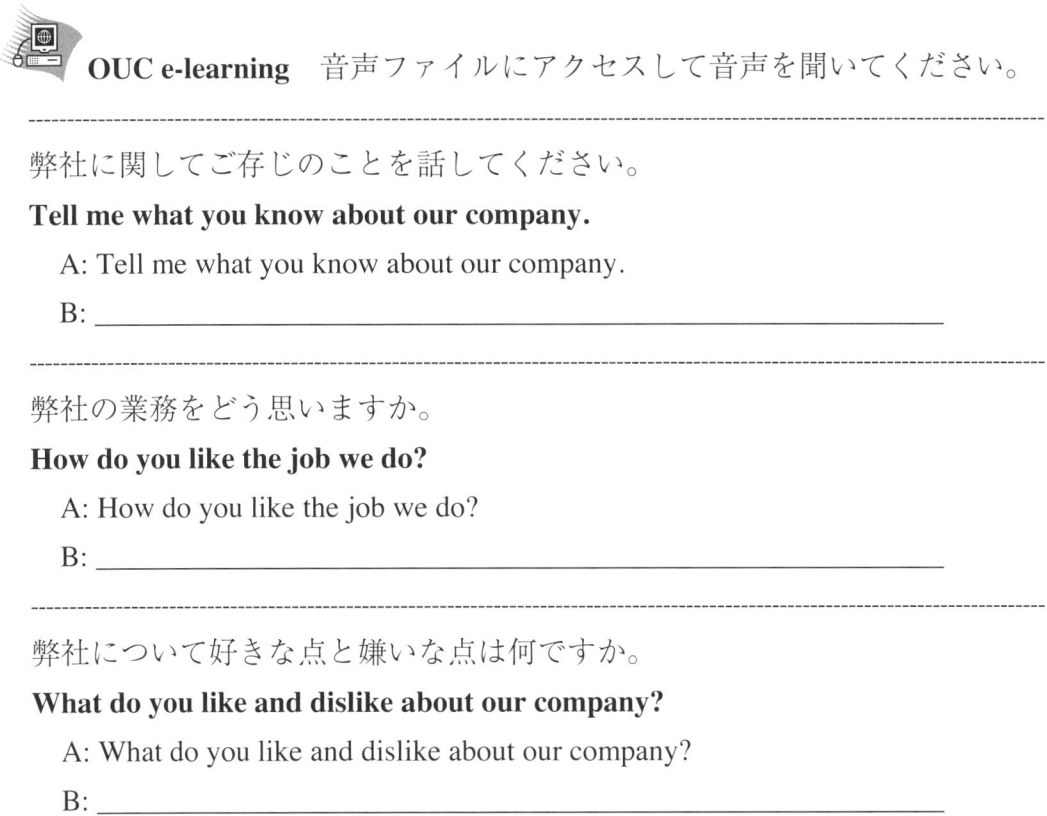

OUC e-learning 音声ファイルにアクセスして音声を聞いてください。

弊社に関してご存じのことを話してください。

Tell me what you know about our company.

    A: Tell me what you know about our company.

    B: _____

弊社の業務をどう思いますか。

How do you like the job we do?

    A: How do you like the job we do?

    B: _____

弊社について好きな点と嫌いな点は何ですか。

What do you like and dislike about our company?

    A: What do you like and dislike about our company?

    B: _____

STEP 4: What You Can Do for the Company （会社への貢献）

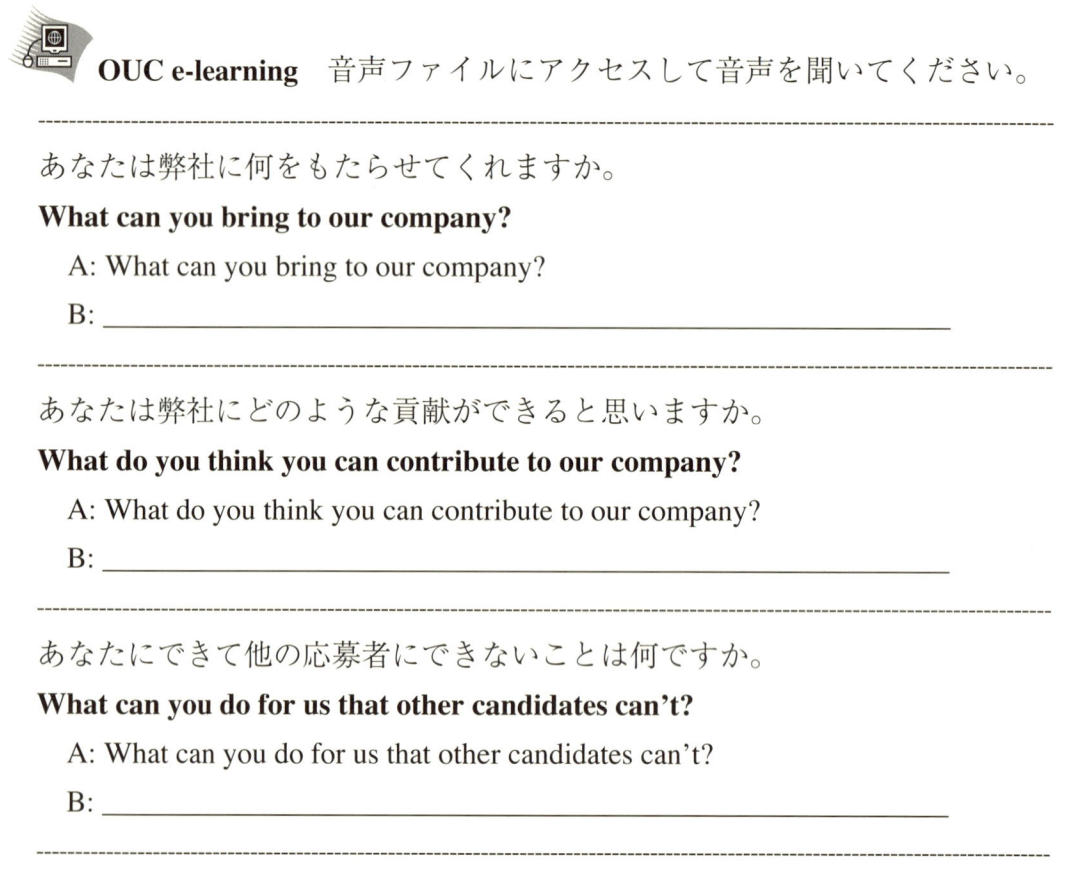

OUC e-learning　音声ファイルにアクセスして音声を聞いてください。

あなたは弊社に何をもたらせてくれますか。

What can you bring to our company?

　　A: What can you bring to our company?

　　B: _____

あなたは弊社にどのような貢献ができると思いますか。

What do you think you can contribute to our company?

　　A: What do you think you can contribute to our company?

　　B: _____

あなたにできて他の応募者にできないことは何ですか。

What can you do for us that other candidates can't?

　　A: What can you do for us that other candidates can't?

　　B: _____

CHAPTER II: Job Hunting

STEP 5: Asking Your Background（バックグラウンドを聞く）

OUC e-learning　音声ファイルにアクセスして音声を聞いてください。

ご自身のことと経歴についてお話しください。
Tell me about yourself and your background.
    A: Tell me about yourself and your background.
    B: _____

自分自身を３つの言葉で表してください。
What three words would you use to describe yourself?
    A: What three words would you use to describe yourself?
    B: _____

大学では何を勉強されましたか。
What did you study at college?
    A: What did you study at college?
    B: _____

STEP 6: Asking Your Expertise（特技、技能を聞く）

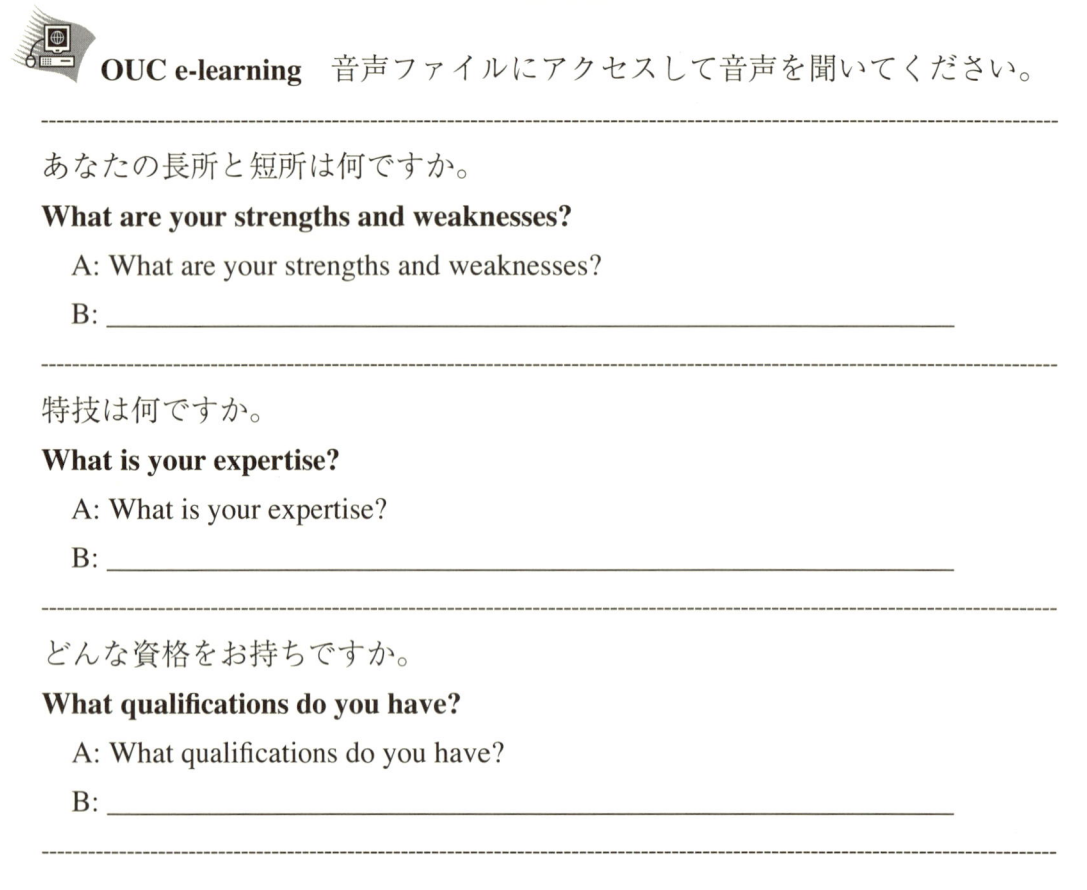

OUC e-learning　音声ファイルにアクセスして音声を聞いてください。

あなたの長所と短所は何ですか。

What are your strengths and weaknesses?

   A: What are your strengths and weaknesses?

   B: _____

特技は何ですか。

What is your expertise?

   A: What is your expertise?

   B: _____

どんな資格をお持ちですか。

What qualifications do you have?

   A: What qualifications do you have?

   B: _____

CHAPTER II: Job Hunting

STEP 7: Job Preferences （仕事の好み）

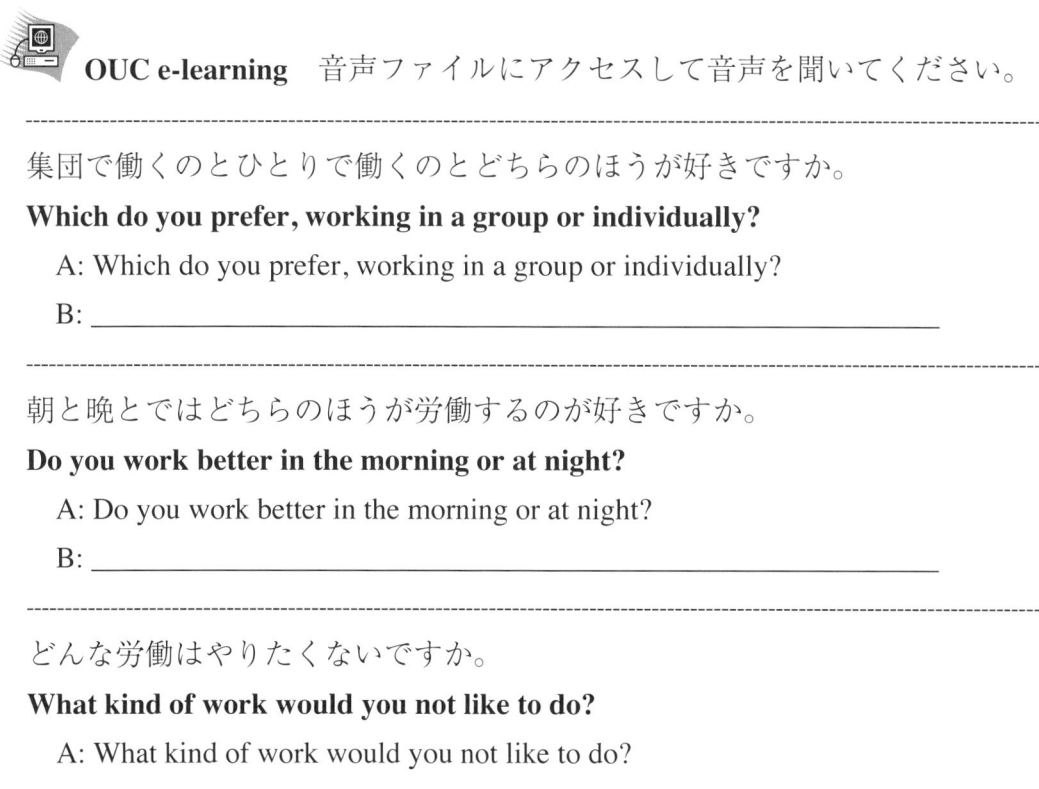

OUC e-learning　音声ファイルにアクセスして音声を聞いてください。

集団で働くのとひとりで働くのとどちらのほうが好きですか。

Which do you prefer, working in a group or individually?

　　A: Which do you prefer, working in a group or individually?

　　B: _____

朝と晩とではどちらのほうが労働するのが好きですか。

Do you work better in the morning or at night?

　　A: Do you work better in the morning or at night?

　　B: _____

どんな労働はやりたくないですか。

What kind of work would you not like to do?

　　A: What kind of work would you not like to do?

　　B: _____

STEP 8: Your Career Goals （将来の目標）

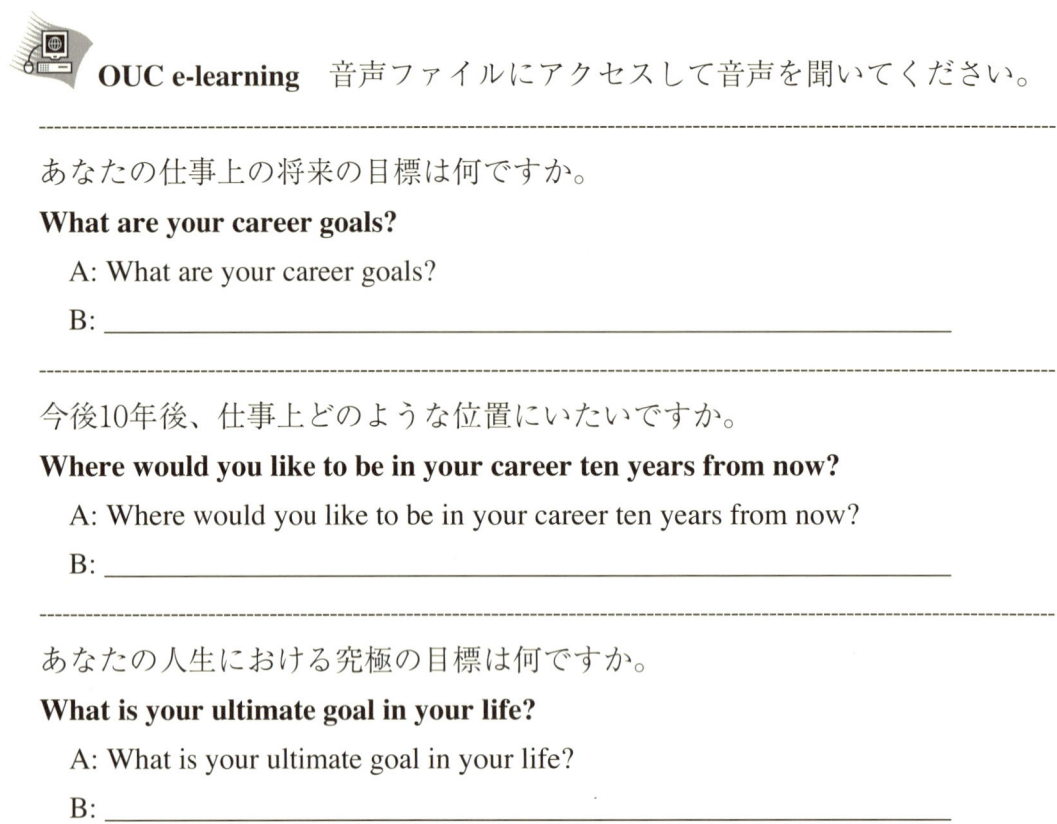

OUC e-learning　音声ファイルにアクセスして音声を聞いてください。

あなたの仕事上の将来の目標は何ですか。

What are your career goals?

 A: What are your career goals?

 B: _____

今後10年後、仕事上どのような位置にいたいですか。

Where would you like to be in your career ten years from now?

 A: Where would you like to be in your career ten years from now?

 B: _____

あなたの人生における究極の目標は何ですか。

What is your ultimate goal in your life?

 A: What is your ultimate goal in your life?

 B: _____

CHAPTER III

Service Encounters

UNIT 1: Working at a Souvenir Shop

STEP 1: Serving Customers

　あなたは小樽運河沿いにある土産店ビリケンショップ・マイケルでバイトを始めることになりました。店内は、ガラス製品、Ｔシャツ、記念品、菓子類で満たされています。そこへ日本語がまったく話せないが英語がある程度話せるロシア人観光客が大挙してやって来ました。しっかり英語を使って接客してみましょう。マイケル社長からは客との値段交渉は自由にしてよいと言われています。まず、ペアワープで空欄に自分なりの英文を入れてみましょう。

A Dialog at Billiken Shop Michael

A: Hello. May I help you?
B: No, thanks. I'm just looking.
A: Please tell me when you need my help.
B: Thank you.
A: Hello. Are you looking for something?
C: Yes, I'm looking for something that represents Otaru.
A: Represents Otaru? Oh, then, definitely, the canal. How about this T-shirt?
C: What do the Chinese characters say?
A: They say "Otaru Canal with love."
C: Sounds great! How much is it?
A: **They are 3 for 5,000 yen.**
C: I want _____. How much is one shirt?
A: It's _____ yen. So **your total will be _____ yen.**
C: Can you give me a better price?
A: Yes, how about _____?
C: Well, could you make it cheaper?
A: How about _____?
C: Okay, I'll take them.
A: Thank you, sir. How would you like to pay? Cash or charge?
C: Traveler's check.
A: Sure.
C: Here you go.
A: Thank you very much. Please come again.

STEP 2: Substitution Drill （置き換えドリル）

空欄を入れ替えてセンテンス全体を復唱しましょう。

1. It's _____ for _____ yen.　　_____（数量）で_____円です。
   - ⇒ 2　1,000
   - ⇒ 3　2,000
   - ⇒ 4　3,000
   - ⇒ 5　4,000
   - ⇒ 6　5,000

2. Your total will be _____ yen.　合計で_____円になります。
   - ⇒ 2,500
   - ⇒ 4,950
   - ⇒ 8,756
   - ⇒ 12,504
   - ⇒ 32,600

CHAPTER III: Service Encounters

STEP 3: Explaining about Products

土産品について詳しく聞いてくる観光客がいます。製造元や原材料などさまざまな質問がなされます。e-learningにアクセスして対話文を聞き、英文の空欄に適切な語句を入れて完成させてください。

OUC e-learning　音声ファイルにアクセスして音声を聞いてください。

1	製造国を聞かれる	A: Where is it _____? B: It's _____ in Japan.
2	原材料を聞かれる	A: What is it made _____? B: It's made _____ shell.
3	一番売れる時期を聞かれる	A: When does it _____ most? B: August 1st.
4	大きさを聞かれる	A: What is the _____? B: It's a medium.
5	重さを聞かれる	A: What is the _____? B: It's 600 grams.
6	調理法を聞かれる	A: How should it be _____? B: You can boil or grill it.
7	客層を聞かれる	A: What _____ of people mostly buy it? B: Both young and old.
8	年間生産量を聞かれる	A: How many are made in _____? B: Only 500 pieces.
9	返品可能か聞かれる	A: Can it be_____? B: Sure, even if you have used it.
10	在庫があるか聞かれる	A: Are there more in _____? B: Sorry, that's all we have here.

STEP 4: Dealing with Problems

　店内に迷惑な客がいます。日本の風習や常識に明るくない観光客の迷惑行為をどうにかしなければならない場合があります。それぞれの行為が見られた場合、どう言うのがもっとも適切であるか選んでください。

1	大声でうるさい	A: Shut up, please! B: Be quiet, please! C: Could you keep down?
2	店内で食べ歩く	A: No food or drinks, please! B: Please don't eat here. C: Please refrain from eating here.
3	通路や入口をふさいでいる	A: Get lost! B: Could you go away? C: Could you move away?
4	手を触れる	A: Don't touch it. B: Please don't touch it, C: Please keep your hands off.
5	店内を撮影している	A: Don't take a picture here. B: You can't take a picture here. C: No pictures, please.
6	万引きをしている	A: Don't shoplift! B: What are you doing? C: Do you know what you're doing?
7	勝手に試着している	A: Don't try it on. B: You can't try it on. C: You are not allowed to try it on.
8	喫煙しながら店内を歩いている	A: No smoking, please! B: You can't smoke here! C: This is a non-smoking area.
9	騒ぐ我が子に注意しない	A: Please control your kid. B: Please do something about your kid. C: Could you tell your child to keep down, please?
10	家庭ゴミを捨てようとしている	A: No household garbage. B: No trash from home. C: Not for household trash.

CHAPTER III: Service Encounters

STEP 5: When Trouble Happens

なにか店で問題が起きたようです。これは実際に日本で起きた逸話を元に作られた対話文です。対話をよく聞いて、以下のタスクを順に行ってください。

OUC e-learning　音声ファイルにアクセスして音声を聞いてください。

TASK 1: EPISODE A

(1) LISTENING FOR COMPREHENSION

First Listening: Q&A

Q: Where is this conversation taking place?

A: _____.

Second Listening: Multiple Choice

1) What did the customer try on?
   (A) A coat.
   (B) A dress.
   (C) A shirt.

2) How does the customer respond to the sales clerk's request?
   (A) She accepted it.
   (B) She refused it.
   (C) She considered it.

Third Listening: True or False

それぞれの英文が対話文の内容に一致していればT，一致していなかったり言及がなければFを選んでください。

1) The sales clerk did not notice the customer wore strong perfume.　(T / F)
2) The sales clerk thought the customer would take care of the damage. (T / F)
3) The sales clerk called the police when the customer left the shop.　(T / F)

(2) LISTENING FOR PERCEPTION

もう一度同じ対話文を聞いて聞き取った語句を選ぶか、空欄に聞き取った語句を書き入れてください。

OUC e-learning　音声ファイルにアクセスして音声を聞いてください。

A: Can I (**1:** _____) this on?

B: Sure. Please use the dressing room over there.

A: Thank you.

B: Does it (**2:** _____) you?

A: Yes, but I don't like the color.

B: Sorry, but it is the only color (**3:** _____) here.

A: I see.

B: Excuse me, ma'am. I hate to say this, but your perfume has damaged this fur coat.

A: What do you mean?

B: This fur coat cannot be (**4:** _____) any more.

A: So?

B: So I would like you to take care of this damage or buy it.

A: Why should I?

B: Could you pay for this?

A: No way! It's not my (**5:** _____). You should have told me before I tried it on.

B: Yes, but I didn't know you (**6:** _____) such strong perfume.

A: No, no, no! I will not pay! It's your (**7:** _____).

B: Wait! Come back!

TASK 2: EPISODE B

(1) LISTENING FOR COMPREHENSION

対話文を聞いて以下のタスクを行ってください。

OUC e-learning 音声ファイルにアクセスして音声を聞いてください。

First Listening: Q&A

Q: Where is this conversation taking place?

A: _____.

Second Listening: Multiple Choice

1: What did the customer try to do?

    (A) Exchange money.

    (B) Pay in dollars.

    (C) Pay by credit.

2: How does the customer respond to the sales clerk's request?

    (A) He gave up.

    (B) He wouldn't give up.

    (C) He left the shop.

Third Listening: True or False

それぞれの英文が対話文の内容に一致していればT，一致していなかったり言及がなければFを選んでください。

1)	The sales clerk was patiently serving the customer.	(T / F)
2)	The sales clerk was getting scared of the customer.	(T / F)
3)	The sales clerk decided to call the police.	(T / F)

(2) LISTENING FOR PERCEPTION

対話文を聞いて聞き取った語句を選ぶか、空欄に聞き取った語句を書き入れるか選んでください。

OUC e-learning　音声ファイルにアクセスして音声を聞いてください。

A: Good evening. (**1**: _____) yen, sir.

B: How much in dollars?

A: Dollars?

B: I want to pay in dollars.

A: Sorry, but we don't accept any foreign (**2**: _____).

B: Why?

A: That's (**3**: a / the / φ) rule. Please pay in yen.

B: I haven't (**4**: _____) any money yet. I just got into (**5**: _____).

A: I'm sorry.

A: Do you accept cards?

B: No, sir. We accept cash only.

A: Then you should accept dollars!

B: No, we can't.

A: My people are waiting for water. I need to get water for them.

B: I understand your (**6**: _____), but we can't accept dollars.

A: It's midnight. The banks are closed. I can't (**7**: _____) money. Please!

B: No!

CHAPTER III: Service Encounters

STEP 6: What's Wrong with the Signs?

著者（小林）が日本国内で撮影した観光施設、店舗、ホテルの英文の看板があります。それぞれ問題があります。修正してください。

	画像	英文	間違いを指摘してください
1		One's feet attention! （砂川市）	
2		A PIECE OF SUSHI START FROM 72 YEN （札幌市中央区）	
3		May I ask a favor. Please refrain from bring unchecked goods. （札幌市厚別区）	
4		A bus platform for Otaru University of Commerce （小樽市稲穂）	
5		Don't parking without the permission. （札幌市中央区）	

6		Group: More than 20 people （札幌市中央区）	
7		IF YOU CAN OPENED RINGING EMERGENCY ALARM （東京新宿区）	
8		Ticket saling time. （札幌市中央区）	
9		Put on preparing water and tea drink in that corner （北海道虻田郡洞爺村）	
10		do any other unauthorized activities in the any part of the station premises （JR札幌駅）	

CHAPTER III: Service Encounters

UNIT 2: Working at a Restaurant

STEP 1: Fast Food Restaurant

　ファーストフードレストランは、"fast food restaurant"です。"first food restaurant"ではありません。注文のやり取りにはきまったパターンがあります。また、聞き取れなくても写真付きのメニューなどがあれば問題ありません。以下典型的な注文場面の流れですが、日本語を参考に空欄に語句を入れてください。対話文を聞いて、空欄を埋めてください。

OUC e-learning　音声ファイルにアクセスして音声を聞いてください。

Clerk	Hi, may I _____ you?	ご注文をどうぞ。
Customer	Yes, I'd like to _____ coffee and a chicken burger.	はい、コーヒーとチキンバーガーをお願いします。
Clerk	Is that _____, sir?	以上ですか。
Customer	Ah, French fries, too.	ああ、フライドポテトも。
Clerk	For here or to _____?	店内でお召上がりですか、お持ち帰りですか。
Customer	To _____.	持ち帰りで。
Clerk	_____ be 650 yen.	650円になります。
Customer	Here.	はい。
Clerk	Thank you. Here is your _____.	ありがとうございます。おつりです。

91

STEP 2: Sushi Restaurant

　小樽と言えば、寿司ですね。まずは、お馴染みの寿司ネタを英語で言えるかどうかチェックしてみましょう。左にあるそれぞれの寿司ネタを表す英語を右から選んで線で結んでください。

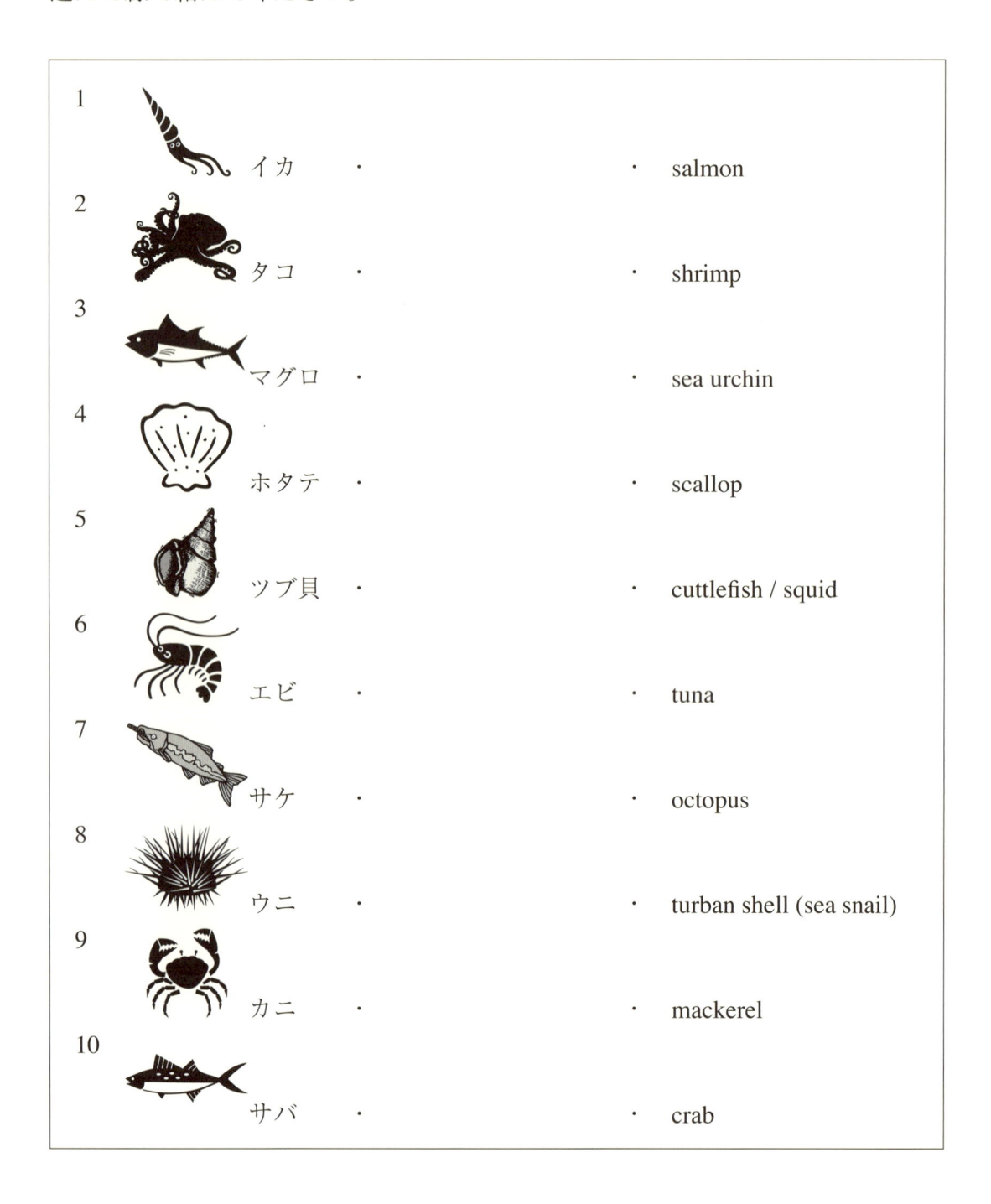

1	イカ	・	salmon
2	タコ	・	shrimp
3	マグロ	・	sea urchin
4	ホタテ	・	scallop
5	ツブ貝	・	cuttlefish / squid
6	エビ	・	tuna
7	サケ	・	octopus
8	ウニ	・	turban shell (sea snail)
9	カニ	・	mackerel
10	サバ	・	crab

STEP 3: Taking an Order at a Japanese Food Restaurant

寿司、天ぷら、そばまで揃えた和食のレストランであなたはウエイター・ウエイトレスをしていると想像してください。ファーストフードレストランのような単純なパターンでは済まされない場合があります。ここでは和食に馴染みが薄い外国人観光客がいろいろと料理の内容について詳しく聞いてくる様子を想定して、ペアでロールプレイをしてください。まずは対話文を聞いて聞き取った語句を空欄に入れてから、ペアワークで、空欄に自由な語句を入れてください。

OUC e-learning　音声ファイルにアクセスして音声を聞いてください。

Waiter	May I take your order?	ご注文をお伺いしてもよろしいですか。
Customer	Yes, what is _____?	はい、_____とは何ですか。
Waiter	It's a kind of _____.	一種の_____です。
Customer	What does it taste like?	どんな味がしますか。
Waiter	It tastes like_____.	_____のような味がします。
Customer	Sounds good. I'll have it.	うまそうだね。それをもらおうか。
Waiter	Thank you, sir [ma'am]. Would you like something to drink?	ありがとうございます。お飲みものがいかがですか。
Customer	Yes, what drink goes well with the food?	はい、この料理に合うのは何かな？
Waiter	I recommend _____, sir [ma'am].	_____がよろしいかと存じます。
Customer	Great! I'll take it.	いいね。それにしよう。

STEP 4: Making Menus & Notices

バイト先の和食料理屋のご主人から外国人観光客向けメニューとして、店内の表示を英語で書いてもらうよう頼まれました。もちろん、ボーナスも出るそうです。がんばって作ってみましょう。

A. Menus

それぞれのメニューに対して、英文名を付けてください。さらに、材料や調理法などを含む簡単な説明を数行書いてください。さらに、値段も付けてください。

和名	英名	説明	値段
もずく酢			yen
きんぴらごぼう			yen
いわしのつみれ汁			yen
湯豆腐			yen
うな丼			yen

CHAPTER III: Service Encounters

B. Notices

店内に英文の注意書きを貼ることになりました。以下実在する和文の注意書きを英文に訳してください。

	Notices	Translate into English.
1	ご注意下さい。扉が、突然 開きます。	
2	衝突注意！このドアは開くことがあります。	
3	人間以外立入り禁止 第9地区 4/10	
4	喫煙所はございません。全面禁煙 お客さまのご理解とご協力を	
5	頭上からの鳩糞注意	

95

STEP 5: Listening to a Recipe

　ある国の料理の調理の過程を説明した英語のナレーションを聞き取ってください。何度も聞いて、以下の表に聞き取った情報を書き入れてください。次に、この料理についてペアまたはグループで以下のような質問をし合ってください：

OUC e-learning　音声ファイルにアクセスして音声を聞いてください。

Have you ever eaten this food?
How do you like this food?
Would you like to make this food?

Name of Food 料理名	
Ingredients 材料	
Seasoning 調味料	
Cooking Utensils 調理具	
Method of Cooking 調理法	

STEP 6: Cooking Vocabulary

1	材料を準備する **prepare**	wash = ～を洗う / wash rice = 米を研ぐ / peel = ～の皮を手でむく / pare = ～の皮を刃物でむく / soak in water to reconstitute = ～を水で戻す / dip into water = ～を水に漬ける / rinse = ～をゆすぐ / drain = ～の水を切る
2	材料を切る **cut**	cut = ～を切る / cut into halves = ～を半分に切る / cut into fourths = ～を四割にする / cut into eight pieces = ～を八割にする / cut into cubes = ～を角切りにする / cut into slices = ～を薄く切る / cut into fine strips = ～を千切りにする / cut into a thin sheet = ～をかつらむきにする / shave = ～を笹切りする / cut into flower shapes = ～を花切りにする / mince = ～をみじん切りにする / cut into rings = ～を輪切りにする / cut into crescents = ～を半月切りにする / round slice and then quarter = ～をイチョウ切りにする / cut into dice = ～をさいの目切りにする / grate = ～をおろす / mash = ～をすりつぶす / grind = ～を挽く / tear into pieces = ～をちぎる
3	加熱する **cook**	cook = ～を調理する / heat = ～を温める / boil = ～をゆでる / simmer = ～を弱火で煮る / poach = とろ火で煮る / boil at high heat = ～を強火で煮る / braise = ～を揚げ煮する / stew = ～を煮込む / boil down = ～を煮詰める / steam = ～を蒸す
4	焼く **bake**	bake = ～をオーブンで焼く / roast = ～をあぶって焼く / roast on a skewer = ～を串焼きにする / broil; grill = ～を直火で焼く / barbecue = ～を味付けして焼く / roast whole = ～を丸焼きする / toast = ～をきつね色に焼く / fry = ～を炒める、～を揚げる / deep fry = ～を揚げる

UNIT 3: Expressing Whatever You Want

STEP 1: Communication Strategies

　日常の会話の中で特定の言葉を失念したり、適切な言葉が見つけられないことは誰もが母語でも経験します。外国語においてはそれは頻繁に起きる現象です。外国語の場合、母語では言えるが目標言語 (TL: Target Language)では言い表せない、訳語がわからない場合どうするか。その対処の仕方は総じてコミュニケーション方略 (communication strategies) と呼ばれています。

　例えば、「水族館」を英語でどう言ってよいのかわからなかった場合、主要な対処法としては、言語学者Biakystok (1983)という言語学者が命名した word coinage（造語）と言語学者Tarone (1977)が命名したcircumlocution（定義）というのがあります。前者は、目標言語（学習言語）に存在しない語彙項目を発話者がその対象物を表すに適切と判断する新しい語句をその場で即興で作り上げる方略です。新語と言っても存在しない単語を作り上げるのではなく、既成の語句を使って意味ある新たな組み合わせをします。例えば、「水族館」を fish zoo（魚の動物園）/ marine zoo（海洋動物園）/ museum of fish（魚の博物館）などということができます。いずれも辞書には出ていない表現ですが、何のことを指しているか察することができます。ただし、新語を創造することができれば自分のメッセージを伝えることができますが、学習者は同じ新語を使い続けるのではなく、その後に辞書等でしっかりと単語を調べておくことが望ましいです。

　既成の単語を組み合わせた名詞句 (noun phrase)で伝えたい語彙項目を表現するのが造語ですが、関係節 (relative clause)などの修飾節を駆使してもっと長い単位で表現するのがcircumlocution（定義）で、paraphrasingと呼ばれることもあります。これは英英辞書の定義文のようなもので、「水族館」は、place where you can see a lot of fish in tanksと表すことができます。これはまさに英英辞書に出ている定義文そのものです。適切な語彙項目が頭に浮かばなくても、How can I get to the place where you can see a lot of fish in tanks?と言えば目的が達成できます。もちろん、補足的にYou know, the building you pay at the entrance and see a variety of fish displayed to visitors inside.などの道案内を引き出すまで懸命に続けることも必要かも知れません。このようにa place whereという関係副詞節を使うことであらゆる場所や建物がそのものずばりを言い表す単語を知らなくても通じるのです。

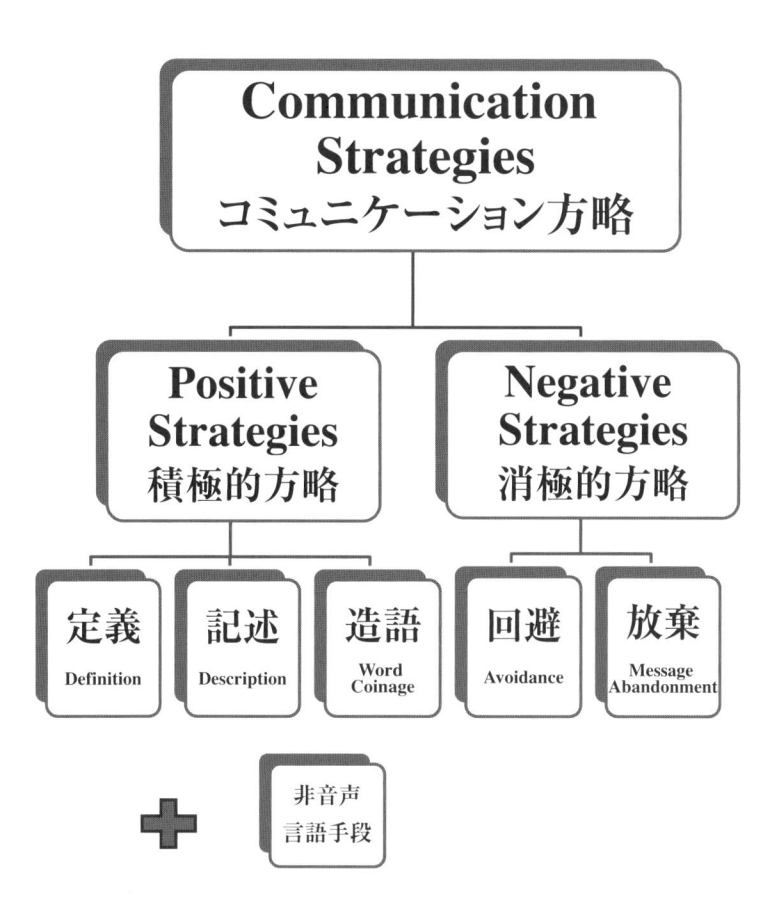

Communication Strategies
コミュニケーション方略

```
Communication Strategies
コミュニケーション方略
├── Positive Strategies 積極的方略
│   ├── 定義 Definition
│   ├── 記述 Description
│   └── 造語 Word Coinage
└── Negative Strategies 消極的方略
    ├── 回避 Avoidance
    └── 放棄 Message Abandonment

+ 非音声言語手段
```

STEP 2: Word Matching

左にあるそれぞれの語句を表した定義を右から選んで線で結んでください。

1. post office ·	· something to pay to get goods and services
2. tax ·	· an artificial waterway to connect places
3. saw ·	· a rising or falling surface
4. Saturn ·	· hard and colorless material
5. I.D. card ·	· a card that shows who you are
6. folklore ·	· a reduction in prices
7. canal ·	· money you pay to the government
8. slope ·	· a story that starts with "A long time ago"
9. glass ·	· money you pay for education
10. money ·	· money you gain from selling something
11. octopus ·	· fixed regular pay each month for a job
12. bank ·	· agreement to pay money in case of accidents
13. salary ·	· a person who starts a business
14. insurance ·	· a statement intended to explain a fact or event
15. profit ·	· a state of being unable to pay one's debts
16. tuition ·	· a place where you can buy stamps
17. discount ·	· a tool you use to cut wood
18. bankruptcy ·	· a place where money is kept and paid out
19. theory ·	· a sea animal that has eight legs
20. entrepreneur ·	· a planet that has rings around it

STEP 3: Creative Framework

　STEP2の定義に見られるよう、さまざまな表し方があります。次のページにある図表は、著者がCF（Creative Framework）と呼ぶ、定義で使用されるパターンをまとめたものです。CFは単なる図表に終わらせず、この設計図に合わせて発話できるように実際に言ってみることが大切です。CFは以下の手順で活用できます。

　第1に話者は、その表そうとするもののエッセンスを正確に捉えた核の部分を特定しなければなりません。「台所」ならまず、placeかspaceを選んで、次に関係詞を選びa place whereを作ります。この名詞の選択が一番大切で、CFのコアになる部分です。

　第2に前修飾部にその空間に対するイメージを表す修飾語を前に付けて、後修飾部の関係詞等を選んでa small place whereを完成させ、そこで行われている行為を一般主語を用いて表し後修飾部を充実させて、最終的にa small place where people cook somethingを完成させます。名詞のみならず、「垢を擦る」という行為なら、コアはactionを選びan action to take away dirt on the skinのように後修飾部は不定詞の形容詞的用法を用いて不定詞句を続けることができます。

　関係節のみならず、a tool used to make …のように動詞の過去分詞の形容詞的用法を使ったパターンや、a tool to ….のように不定詞の形容詞用法や、a tool you use to …のような不定詞の副詞的用法を用いたパターンもあります。ものによってはこれらのいずれかのパターンでも表せるものもあります。例えば、saw（のこぎり）の場合には、以下のように表すことができます：

　　(1)　a tool you use when you want to cut trees　　関係節
　　(2)　a tool you use to cut trees　　関係節＋不定詞の副詞的用法
　　(3)　a tool to cut trees　　不定詞の形容詞的用法

　いずれも使えるようにしておくと便利です。このＣＦをマスターすれば、例えその単語を知らなくても、なにかの商品を説明したりできるようになるだけでなく、森羅万象なんでも言い表せるようになるはずです。語彙力が足りないなどと悲観していてはいけません。胸を張って自信を持ってなんでも英語で言い表してみましょう！

Creative Framework

限定詞	形容詞	名詞（コア）	後修飾部
φ	large	place	who is
a	huge	area	who does
an	small	zone	who did
the	tiny	region	who has
some	middle-sized	country	who likes to
a kind of	strong	room	who is likely to
a sort of	weak	part	who is subject to
	wild	creature	who can
	dangerous	animal	who used to
	scary	plant	
	common	organ	which is
	widespread	food	which does
	well-known	drink	which did
	famous	vehicle	which has
	popular	building	which is likely
	familiar	structure	which is subject to
	unfamiliar	thing	which can
	rare	something	which used to
	precious	item	
	valuable	stuff	that is
	important	substance	that does（過去の一般動詞）
	unimportant	material	that did（過去の一般動詞）
	strange	symbol	
	unusual	object	that has
	normal	design	that is likely
	abnormal	mark	that is subject to
	useful	sign	that can
	helpful	pattern	that used to
	convenient	shape	
	inconvenient	figure	whose …….
	beautiful	geography	
	pretty	measure	to不定詞（形容詞的用法）
	ugly	approach	
	deformed	machine	過去分詞の形容詞的用法 (used to / designed toなど)
	expensive	appliance	
	inexpensive	device	
	cheap	tool	現在分詞の形容詞的用法
	chemical	event	
	biological	chance	
	nuclear	opportunity	
	natural	occasion	
	unnatural	phenomenon	
	supernatural	time	
	spiritual	day	
	mysterious	behavior	
	dangerous	custom	
	risky	tradition	
	explosive	system	
		ceremony	
		clothes	
		person [people]	
		occupation	
		work [job]	
		means [method]	
		way	

CHAPTER III: Service Encounters

STEP 4: Guess What I Mean

以下接客に関する言葉を定義したものです。何を表しているのか当ててください。解答を空間に、英語または日本語で書き入れてください。

1	a promise to use a service, like eating at a table and staying at a hotel	
2	a person who carries food and drinks to tables at a restaurant	
3	a card to be used as money to buy goods and services	
4	money customers give to someone who has served them well	
5	messages to invite customers written on paper or in another medium	
6	action to reduce prices of goods and services for customers who ask them	
7	a list of food and drinks available in restaurants	
8	a famous Japanese consisting food of a piece of rice topped with fish	
9	a system that makes people enjoy singing along any songs they choose	
10	a tool to pick up and eat food by a hand	

STEP 5: Express Yourself

　以下ビジネスに関する言葉を自分なりに英語で定義して、空間に書き入れてください。または、それをペアワークでパートナーに口頭で伝えて、何を表しているのか当ててもらってください。ここに出ていない言葉でも構いません。

1	土産	
2	時給	
3	昇進	
4	ボーナス	
5	就職活動	
6	適性	
7	契約書	
8	解雇	
9	アポイントメント	
10	企画	

CHAPTER IV

Presentation

UNIT 1: What is a Presentation?

STEP 1: Understanding Presentations

　プレゼンテーションとは何かご存じですか。スピーチとどう違うのでしょうか。日本語では単に「発表」と訳されますが、訳さずそのまま「プレゼンテーション」または短く「プレゼン」と言うことが多いです。今日でもプレゼンテーションとは、一般的に「何かしっかりと調べてきたものをパワーポイントなどのソフトを資料にして資料の効果的な提示と共に聴衆に報告したり、説得力ある説明をする行為」と定義されます。プレゼンテーションは、何かを多数の相手に伝える行為としてスピーチの一種と考えられますが、その場で即興でできる単なる挨拶や激励などと異なり、時間をかけてリサーチし、報告するものです。

　民間企業、官公庁、学校、研究機関では今日もっともポピュラーなプレゼンテーションと言えば、特定の時間内に複数の聴衆を相手に、パソコンのパワーポイントというコンピュータ・プログラムで作成した図表やリストを掲載したスライドを効果的に一枚一枚提示しながら説明を淡々と進め、発表最中や終了後に聴衆からの質問に回答する形態です。基本的に何か資料等を調べるリサーチを行い、取得した情報や数値を図形やグラフにまとめて提示します。かつて主流だったOHP（Overhead Projector）やホワイトボードよりも、視覚的にはより多くの情報が効果的に提示できるパワーポイントを使用したプレゼンテーションが主流になっています。

　プレゼンテーションの重要性は特にビジネス・シーンでは近年ますます高まってきており、商談での交渉力と並んで重要なビジネス・スキルのひとつとして広く認識されています。営業担当者だけでなく、技術者も自らの研究開発した製品やサービスを発表する時代です。企業に就職する人も、公務員になる人も、研究者になる人も、プレゼンテーションを行う機会はますます増えてきています。こうした社会の需要に応え日本の多くの大学でプレゼンテーション能力がますます重要視されてきています。英語の授業だけでなく、一般の授業やゼミの中で学生に発表の機会を積極的に与えるところが増えてきています。

　CHAPTER IVでは、英語によるプレゼンテーションの準備ためのスピーチの書き方が英語で解説されています。日本語による日本語のスピーチの作成法並びにパワーポイントのスライド画面の作成法は付録に掲載しているので参考にしてください。

STEP 2: The Difference between Classroom Presentations and Business Presentations

Class presentations, such as those in your English classes, are often good practice for presentations in business. But, only if you can overcome the problems that so many students have with classroom presentations (hesitations, lack of confidence, inaccurate information, poor speaking style, etc.). It is important to remember that if you fail in a classroom presentation the worst that might happen is you may fail the assignment or the class. In business, a failed presentation could mean the loss of a contract and could cost your company a lot of money.

In this chapter we will look at what makes a good presentation, and will construct a business presentation step by step.

参考サイト

Classroom Presentation
   http://www.youtube.com/watch?v=VjivbXW8S9U&feature=related
Business Presentations
   http://www.youtube.com/watch?v=IFOfyG4WVAM
   http://www.youtube.com/watch?v=X5yRhOSL_-c&feature=related

STEP 3: Common Mistakes Made by Students in Classroom Presentations

1. Hesitations and pauses. This is a sign of lack of preparation.

2. Speaking in monotone. The speaker is boring.

3. Nervousness. It is normal to be nervous during a presentation, but good speakers learn to control this nervousness and therefore perform better.

4. Not engaging the audience. One of the biggest mistakes Japanese speakers make in giving presentations in English is that they fail to look at their audience. The audience will respond much better if they feel you are talking to them, and not to the wall or your paper.

5. Reading directly from the paper. Another problem in Japan. Reading to your audience is unacceptable in any presentation, meeting, or business setting. Your audience is not made up of children. They can read for themselves. Reading serves no one.

6. Not knowing the material. The material you are presenting should not be new to you. Know your material before the presentation.

7. Depending too much on PowerPoint. PowerPoint is a tool, and only a tool. It should not be the presentation itself. Many good speakers know that PowerPoint can be a distraction.

STEP 4: Tips for Successful Business Presentations

1. Know your subject. Come prepared and know your material ahead of time. This means practicing.
2. Speak with confidence. If you are making a business proposal, talking about quarterly sales numbers, or any other business task, people with only listen to you if you speak with authority and confidence.
3. Speak loudly and clearly. Your voice should be able to be understood by everyone there.
4. Learn to vary your voice quality. Show enthusiasm for what you are talking about. Use stress to highlight important points. The more engaging you are to your audience the more success you are likely to have.
5. Encourage questions. By encouraging people to ask questions you are showing confidence. Your ability to answer those questions will show your audience your knowledge of the subject.
6. Present your material to us. DON'T READ TO US. Looking occasionally at your notes is fine, but reading page after page of information is not appropriate in business, or in any formal presentation.
7. Talk to us (your audience). Look at us, move your eyes around the room to different participants as you are speaking. Again, this will make the audience feel included in your presentation.
8. If you are using a podium, don't always stand at the podium. Move around on the stage and talk to your audience. Or move over towards the screen (if you are using slides). Standing only at the podium is less interesting and often suggests that the speaker is hiding behind the podium.
9. Limit your use of PowerPoint. Many of the best speakers do not even use PowerPoint. They want the focus on them, not on the slides. Use PowerPoint to assist you, not to overpower you as the speaker. You want the audience to focus on you, not only on the slides.
10. Be prepared for possible questions that participants might ask.
11. If you can't answer a question, that's ok. It's better to say "I don't know." rather than to give a wrong answer. The best speakers will say "I don't know. Let me check that and get back to you."

UNIT 2: Outlining a Successful Presentation

Business presentations, just as with formal writing, requires a strong design. You can use the same outline form you used for essay writing to create a strong business presentation. In this chapter we are going to build a business presentation from introduction to conclusion.

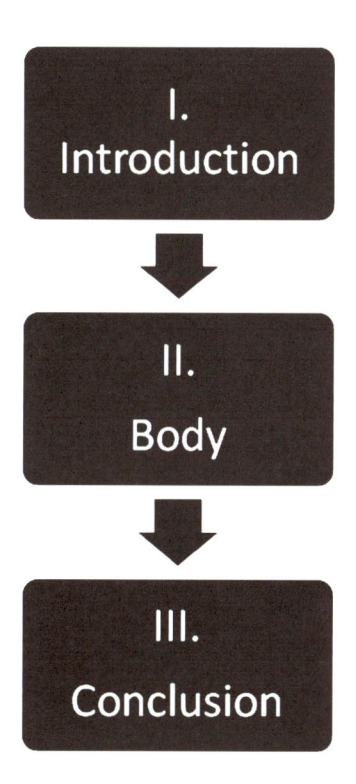

```
I. Introduction
      ↓
II. Body
      ↓
III. Conclusion
```

STEP 1: Deciding Your Subject

In this chapter, you will design a business presentation. First, you will need to decide your topic. For the purposes of this class, let's imagine you are introducing your company (a company you choose) to a potential client (who will be the audience of this class).

Think for a moment about a lesser-known company that you would like to research (or one that you admire and would like to know more about), then write the name of the company on the line below. (Avoid choosing a company everyone knows.)

The company I will research for my presentation is _____.

I: Introduction

Your introduction should cover the following questions.

1. Greeting
2. Who are you?
3. What is the title or purpose of your presentation?
4. Why does this topic need to be discussed?
5. What is your connection to the topic?

Sample Introduction

Hello. It's a pleasure to be here today. For those here who don't know me I'm Bill Davis, Sales Manager for Star Consulting. I'm here today to talk to you about our company's services. As many of you are aware, the past year has been very difficult for many companies. I believe, however, that economic uncertainty can lead to opportunity and I believe that Star Consulting is well positioned to assist your company in reaching its goals. Let me first cover our goals, and then second talk about how we can help you achieve your company's goals in this period of uncertainty.

Useful Phrases and Vocabulary

It's a pleasure to be here today.

For those who don't know me,

I'm here to talk to you about …

As many of you are aware,

Let me first cover,

… and then second talk about …

Your Turn

On the lines below, write a sample introduction for your presentation. Use the sample paragraph and phrases to assist you.

_____
_____
_____

II: Body

In the body section you will make your key points. For this you will need to research your company.

Assignment 1: For the next class, find your company's profile. Often this will be found on the company's website in the introduction or history sections. You should try to find information to answer the following questions:

1: What does your company do?

2: What products does the company offer?

3: What is the company's market share?

4: What is the company's most recent profit report?

5: Other information that you think would be useful to attract new clients (history, etc).

6: Who are the company's major clients?

7: Who are the company's major competitors and how is the company you are representing different?

On the lines below fill in the information you have discovered about your company (background).

Sample Background Section

Please allow me to tell you about our company, Star Consulting. Star Consulting has been in business since 1955 and has been serving companies mainly in the New York and Chicago markets. In 2009, we began to broaden westward and now serve businesses in 48 of 50 states. Last year, we recorded sales in excess of $47,000,000 and this year we expect to continue to grow by roughly 8%. While we are not the largest consulting firm, we believe that we have a more personalized service and a better relationship with each of our customers. Our primary business is consulting to companies on how to streamline operations, increase productivity and to cut overhead. On average, we can normally help our clients to reduce costs by 15% and increase productivity by 20-25%. Our motto expresses our connection to our customers, "When you succeed, we succeed!".

Useful Phrases and Vocabulary

Please allow me to tell you about …

[ ] We now serve businesses in …

[ ] We recorded sales in excess of …

[ ] We expect to continue to grow by …

[ ] While we are not the _____, we believe we _____.

[ ] Our primary business is to …

[ ] On average, we can …

Your Turn

On the lines below write the background part of your body section.

_____
_____
_____
_____
_____
_____
_____
_____

STEP 2: Using Additional Information for Support

Sample paragraph

As I mentioned, since 2009 we have grown greatly and now consult for companies all over mainland America. Some of our major clients include Baxter Pharmaceuticals, Roman Automobiles, and Popsi-Cola. We would be happy to put you in touch with some of our clients who can vouch for our ability to realize cost-savings for your company. We realize that you have a number of choices for consulting firms. While other firms may be larger than ours, we believe that our personalized approach, which involves continuous contact between our company and our client, gives us an edge in service and performance.

Useful Phrases and Vocabulary:

[ ] As I mentioned,

[ ] Some of our major clients include,

[ ] We would be happy to put you in touch with …

[ ] We realize that you have a number of choices in …

Your Turn:

On the lines below write your supporting paragraph.

_____
_____
_____
_____
_____
_____
_____
_____

III. Conclusion

Your conclusion should begin with a closing phrase to let us know that you are nearing the end. Then, you should touch on your key point or points again. Finally, you should leave us with a final statement thanking your audience and calling for questions.

Sample Conclusion:

In closing, let me state again the important numbers I mentioned earlier. On average, we can normally help our clients to reduce costs by 15% and increase productivity by 20-25%. We are confident that if you run the numbers, you will see that we can produce significant improvements for your company. We strongly hope to work with your company and are grateful for the opportunity to present our company's profile to you here today. Thank you.

Now, I would be happy to answer any questions you may have.

Useful Phrases and Vocabulary:

In closing,

let me state again …

We are confident that ...

We strongly hope to work with your company.

I would be happy to answer any questions you may have.

Your Turn:

_____
_____
_____
_____
_____
_____

Assignment 2: Now that you have a rough draft of your presentation. Rewrite the entire presentation on a computer, print it out, and bring it to the next class.

STEP 3: Sample Presentation

> Hello. It's a pleasure to be here today. For those here who don't know me I'm Bill Davis, Sales Manager for Star Consulting. I'm here today to talk to you about our company's services. As many of you are aware, the past year has been very difficult for many companies. I believe, however, that economic uncertainty can lead to opportunity and I believe that Star Consulting is well positioned to assist your company in reaching its goals. Let me first cover our goals, and then second talk about how we can help you achieve your company's goals in this period of uncertainty.
>
> Please allow me to tell you about our company, Star Consulting. Star Consulting has been in business since 1955 and has been serving companies mainly in the New York and Chicago markets. In 2009, we began to broaden westward and now serve businesses in 48 of 50 states. Last year, we recorded sales in excess of $47,000,000 and this year we expect to continue to grow by roughly 8%. While we are not the largest consulting firm, we believe that we have a more personalized service and a better relationship with each of our customers. Our primary business is consulting to companies on how to streamline operations, increase productivity and to cut overhead. On average, we can normally help our clients to reduce costs by 15% and increase productivity by 20-25%. Our motto expresses our connection to our customers, "When you succeed, we succeed!".
>
> As I mentioned, since 2009 we have grown greatly and now consult for companies all over mainland America. Some of our major clients include Baxter Pharmaceuticals, Roman Automobiles, and Popsi-Cola. We would be happy to put you in touch with some of our clients who can vouch for our ability to realize cost-savings for your company. We realize that you have a number of choices for consulting firms. While other firms may be larger than ours, we believe that our personalized approach, which involves continuous contact between our company and our client, gives us an edge in service and performance.
>
> In closing, let me state again the important numbers I mentioned earlier. On average, we can normally help our clients to reduce costs by 15% and increase productivity by 20-25%. We are confident that if you run the numbers, you will see that we can produce significant improvements for your company. We strongly hope to work with your company and are grateful for the opportunity to present our company's profile to you here today. Thank you.
>
> Now, I would be happy to answer any questions you may have.

STEP 4: Tips for Using PowerPoint

1. Do not put too much information onto one slide. Each slide should be visible from anywhere in the room.

2. Do not put all of your information on slides. It makes the speaker irrelevant.

3. Slides are best used for tables and graphs of data or statistics, not for information that is easy to understand.

4. Be prepared to speak without slides in the event that there is an equipment malfunction.

5. Remember, the best speakers don't real PowerPoint. If you are a confident, talented speaker there is really no need for it. For speakers who are less confident, PowerPoint can be a useful tool. But, it is only a tool. The real job is for the speaker. It is his or her job to present the information in a meaningful and entertaining way.

CHAPTER V

Discussion

In this chapter we will look at how to take part in business conversations and meetings, how to negotiate, and finally how to argue and defend your arguments.

CHAPTER V: Discussion

UNIT 1: Japanese & American Ways of Discussion

STEP 1: Differences in Japanese and American Discussion Styles (1)
日米の討論の仕方の違いに関する以下の英文を読んでください。

It is often said that Japanese discussion practices are different from those of Western, particularly American, speakers. But, how are they different? It is often said that Japanese speakers tend to speak in a roundabout fashion. The speaker will eventually get to the point, but often in a general way, sometimes without details that many Western speakers would take for granted. On the other hand, American speakers tend to speak in a linear fashion. What this means is that American speakers prefer a direct approach to a topic. If we hear an American speaker going around a topic in a Japanese manner we will assume they are avoiding telling us something. This is not seen as a good strategy in English, yet it is very common in Japanese.

Similarly, the practice of 根回し or getting everyone's approval before a meeting is not a normal practice in America or other English-speaking settings. The point of a Western meeting is normally to argue out the proposal and the details. It is often frustrating for non-Japanese speakers in Japan who go to meetings expecting to give their opinion only to find that the decisions have already been made.

Another frustration of non-Japanese speakers in Japan is the reluctance by Japanese business people to say clearly yes or no to a proposal. While it may be easily understood by Japanese that this may mean no, if this Japanese approach is taken in America it may mean the loss of a business relationship as Americans will view this unclearness as an indecisive or wishy-washy attitude. It will appear as you are not taking our proposals seriously. The result will rarely be positive in such cases.

In business discussions and negotiations in America it is common to openly question the speaker and to ask why. This may be in great contrast to Japanese business situations where why is rarely asked. As a Japanese speaker of English engaging in business, expect to be asked why.

There is also the issue of logic versus emotion and culture. In Western meetings, the speaker will be expected to argue a point logically and rationally. Emotional arguments, or arguments about tradition or culture, or giving deference to the older members of the group (all common Japanese patterns) will not have much success overseas. When you argue in English we expect your reasons for arguing a point to be reasonable and based in a logical argument. This is sometimes very difficult for Japanese business people who follow a hierarchy and who feel uncomfortable openly arguing a subject in a meeting. This chapter is designed to help overcome some of these problems to prepare business people for the challenges of arguing in English.

STEP 2: Differences in Japanese and American Discussion Styles (2)

日米の討論の仕方の違いをまとめた以下の表を見て、それぞれどういう意味であるかを考えてみてください。

Differences in Japanese and American Discussion Styles

Japanese	American
indirect approach	direct approach
nemawashi	the meeting is the place to argue
argument based in emotion	argument based in logic
attentive to hierarchy	anyone can offer ideas
no clear yes or no	expects clear answers
attentive to culture	culture is less important than the reasons
reluctance to ask why	openly questioning

Useful Phrases and Vocabulary
- [ ] I've called you here today to discuss…
- [ ] The company has decided to …
- [ ] in the current economic environment
- [ ] We can't afford to…
- [ ] Why can't you …?
- [ ] basically
- [ ] We are forced to do the same work for less pay.
- [ ] performance bonuses
- [ ] That's why …
- [ ] in terms of
- [ ] The best workers will be rewarded.
- [ ] Too many workers do less than their share.
- [ ] Look at my numbers.
- [ ] I'm still not sure I like the idea of…
- [ ] I want to thank both of you for your time.

UNIT 2: Practice Discussion

STEP 1: Sample Discussion Dialogue 1

Jane has called for a meeting between herself and Ron and Pete, two employees of the company. She must explain to them that there will be a pay cut.

OUC e-learning　音声ファイルにアクセスして音声を聞いてください。

Jane:	I've called you both here to discuss the company's plan to cut salaries. Basically, the company has decided to cut all staff salaries by 6% this year.
Ron:	Why?
Pete:	Yes. Why?
Jane:	In the current economic environment, we can't afford to continue paying everyone. We must either cut staff or cut salaries.
Pete:	Why can't the company cut other expenses first?
Ron:	Is the President going to take a pay cut as well?
Jane:	The company is trying to cut expenses where it can. And yes, the President is going to take a pay cut of 6% as well.
Pete:	So basically, we are forced to do the same work for less pay.
Jane:	Unfortunately, yes.
Ron:	Our president needs to show real leadership. Cutting everyone's salary isn't fair. Some of us bring much more revenue into the company than others.
Jane:	That's true Ron. That's why the president is going to offer performance bonuses to the top three performers in terms of sales within the company. In other words, the best workers will be rewarded.
Pete:	That's a good policy. There are too many of our workers who do less than their share. Their pay should be cut. But, please look at my numbers. They are always at the top.

Ron: I'm still not sure I like the idea of pay cuts. More waste must be cut from the company.

Jane: We will continue to look for new ways of reducing costs. I want to thank both of you for your time. I must go to a meeting now with our other departments. If you have any further questions, call me.

Ron: Thanks Jane.

Pete: Yes. Thanks Jane.

Assignment 1: In a group of three, practice the dialogue three times. Each time change the role each of you is playing.

Useful Phrases and Vocabulary
- [ ] Let's hear your proposal first.
- [ ] So, imagine a…
- [ ] Does it really say anything about ___?
- [ ] I think ___ will appeal to ___.
- [ ] Good point!
- [ ] My proposal is that…
- [ ] As they ___,
- [ ] It's pretty standard.
- [ ] If we want to stick to what's normal, it's fine.
- [ ] I would like to thank you both for your proposals.
- [ ] I will call you back when I've come to a decision.

CHAPTER V: Discussion

STEP 2: Sample Discussion Dialogue 2

Wayne Barnes, the president of a small sales company has called his two employees into the office to make a proposal for the company's new television commercial.

OUC e-learning 音声ファイルにアクセスして音声を聞いてください。

Wayne: Phil, let's hear your proposal first.

Phil: My suggestion is a play on the company name. Our company name is Barnes Supply. The name Barnes sounds and looks the same as the farm type of barn. So, imagine a commercial showing various barns throughout the area, quiet with no dialogue. At the end of the commercial a voice softly claims "Barnes, everywhere you need them."

Wayne: Interesting. I like the slogan. Angela, what do you think?

Angela: It's peaceful. But, does it really say anything about what we do?

Phil: People know what we sell. I think this commercial will appeal to their nostalgic side.

Wayne: Good point. Angela, let's hear your idea.

Angela: My proposal is that we should three guys pulling into a Barnes Supply store parking lot. As they park, 9 a.m. flashes across the screen and one guy says "I just need to stop in to get some nails." The three guys enter. Then the time flashes across the screen again. It's 11 a.m. The three come out of the store will three carts full of stuff. The same guy speaks again. "I only came in to buy some nails." As the camera shows them from the back, pushing the carts away the narrator comes on and says, "Barnes Supply, yeah we've got nails. And so much more."

Wayne: Ok. Thank you Angela. Your proposal is closer to what we normally do. Phil, what do you think?

Phil: I agree that it's pretty standard. If we want to stick to what's normal, it's fine. If we want something new and innovative, then mine is better.

Wayne: Ok. I would like to thank you both for your proposals. I will call you back in when I've come to a decision.

Phil: Thanks, Wayne.

Angela: Thanks a lot.

Assignment 2: In a group of three, practice the dialogue three times. Each time change the role each of you is playing.

STEP 3: Discussion

In your group, discuss the following topic.

As students, you have probably noticed problems or things you would like to see changed at your university. In your group, discuss proposals for improving your university.

Preparation for a larger group discussion

In a larger group discussion, you must both follow the discussion topic and be able to interject (give your opinion) when it is appropriate. The following are some expressions for saying something during a larger group discussion.

Useful Phrases and Vocabulary

Interjecting
- [ ] I have something to add.
- [ ] I'd like to say something.
- [ ] I'd like to interject.
- [ ] If I could interrupt for a moment,
- [ ] Could I add something?

Agreeing
- [ ] I fully agree.
- [ ] I agree with what _____ just said.
- [ ] I think we are all in agreement.

Disagreeing
- [ ] I'm afraid I can't agree.
- [ ] I'm against that proposal.
- [ ] I must disagree.
- [ ] I don't think that's right.
- [ ] In contrast to what you said, I think _____.

Negotiating
- [ ] Let's see if we can reach a solution.
- [ ] Let's try to find some middle ground.
- [ ] Each side needs to give some ground if we are going to reach an agreement.
- [ ] I think we are close to an agreement.
- [ ] There are still a couple of points we need to iron out.

Getting others' feedback
- [ ] What do you think about ____?
- [ ] How do you feel about ____?
- [ ] What's your opinion of ____?
- [ ] Let's hear from _____.
- [ ] Does anyone have anything to say about ____?
- [ ] Does anyone have anything to add?

STEP 4: Tips for a Group Discussion, Meeting, Conference, or Forum

1. Be prepared. Understand the topic ahead of time if possible, and know what you would like to see if you have the opportunity. The more information you have, the better argument you can make.

2. Winning an argument. To win an argument, you should be able to understand the other side's position well enough to repeat it back to them. But, you should also understand the problems with their position (and your own). If you can repeat their position back to them, and get them to agree, then you can easily present the problems with their proposal and then present yours and win.

3. Speak up. If you have something to say, you have to have the courage to say it. Grumbling about it after the meeting is over does nothing. You must speak up when you have the chance.

Small group discussion	Large group discussion
In a group of 4 or 5 students, discuss the following topic. What are the causes of Japan's long economic slump? Japan has had a weak economy since the bubble burst at the end of the 1980s. What do you think are the causes of this continued slump?	Using the information from your small group discussion, you are now going to have a large group discussion as a class. You should be prepared to agree or disagree with the other groups' ideas and be prepared to give your opinions when there is an opportunity.

STEP 5: Extra Practice

In a small group or as a class discuss the following business topics.

1. University students in many countries go to business schools to learn to run a business. In Japan, most business students only want to work for a company (instead of opening their own business). Why are Japanese business students so afraid to open their own businesses?

MEMO

_____
_____
_____
_____
_____

2. In Japan, students doing job hunting all wear the same navy suits and use the same resume forms. The goal is to be the same. In America, everyone dresses professionally, but in their own style and everyone's resume is unique. What are the benefits and problems of each system? Which do you think is better? Why?

MEMO

_____
_____
_____
_____
_____

3. In Japanese companies, workers are often paid by age and not by their educational achievement (like having a Ph.D.) or their talent. This often means older workers who are often less-skilled (but have experience) are paid more than younger more talented workers (who have less years in the company). Should workers be paid according to age or according to talent? Why?

MEMO

_____
_____
_____
_____
_____

4. In many American companies there are casual Fridays. This means no suits and no ties and workers may come to work in casual clothes such as polo shirts and jeans (comfortable clothes). A few companies do this in Japan, but most don't. Why do you think Japanese companies are reluctant to let their workers dress casually? Do you think they should?

MEMO

_____
_____
_____
_____
_____

5. Japanese companies are frequently very slow to change. In a global business world, companies that are slow to change usually lose out on business. Do you agree that Japanese companies are slow to change? Should they learn to move quicker in the marketplace, or do you think Japanese companies are doing the right thing?

MEMO

_____
_____
_____
_____
_____

6. In Japan, it is often said that "The customer is God." Do you agree with this statement. Give examples to show that this statement is true or false.

MEMO

_____
_____
_____
_____
_____

7. Recently, companies such as Uni-qlo and Rakuten have made the official office language English and have given employees two years to be able to speak English or risk being fired. Do you agree with the policy of English as the official company language? Why or why not? Should employees be fired for not learning English in those companies?

MEMO

_____
_____
_____
_____
_____

8. Is it better to hire employees with no experience (who you can train in your company) or to hire employees who come with a lot of experience (but who may not get along in your company)? Why?

MEMO

_____
_____
_____
_____
_____

9. What are the benefits and problems of working in a large company versus working in a small company? Which is better to work for? Why?

MEMO

___

10. What is "leadership"? Why are so few Japanese people willing to be "leaders"? Who are some examples of good "leaders" in Japan? Why?

MEMO

___

Appendix

Appendix 1
Getting to Know Each Other

　将来のビジネスシーンに備えて、まずは英語で他の学生と知り合いになりましょう。以下のダイアローグをＣＤを聞きながら目を通して下線がある語句をなるべく使うようにして、ペアワークをしてください。相手に何か聞かれたら、ただ答え続けるのではなく、同じ質問を相手に返して、相互に会話のキャッチボールを行うようにしましょう。

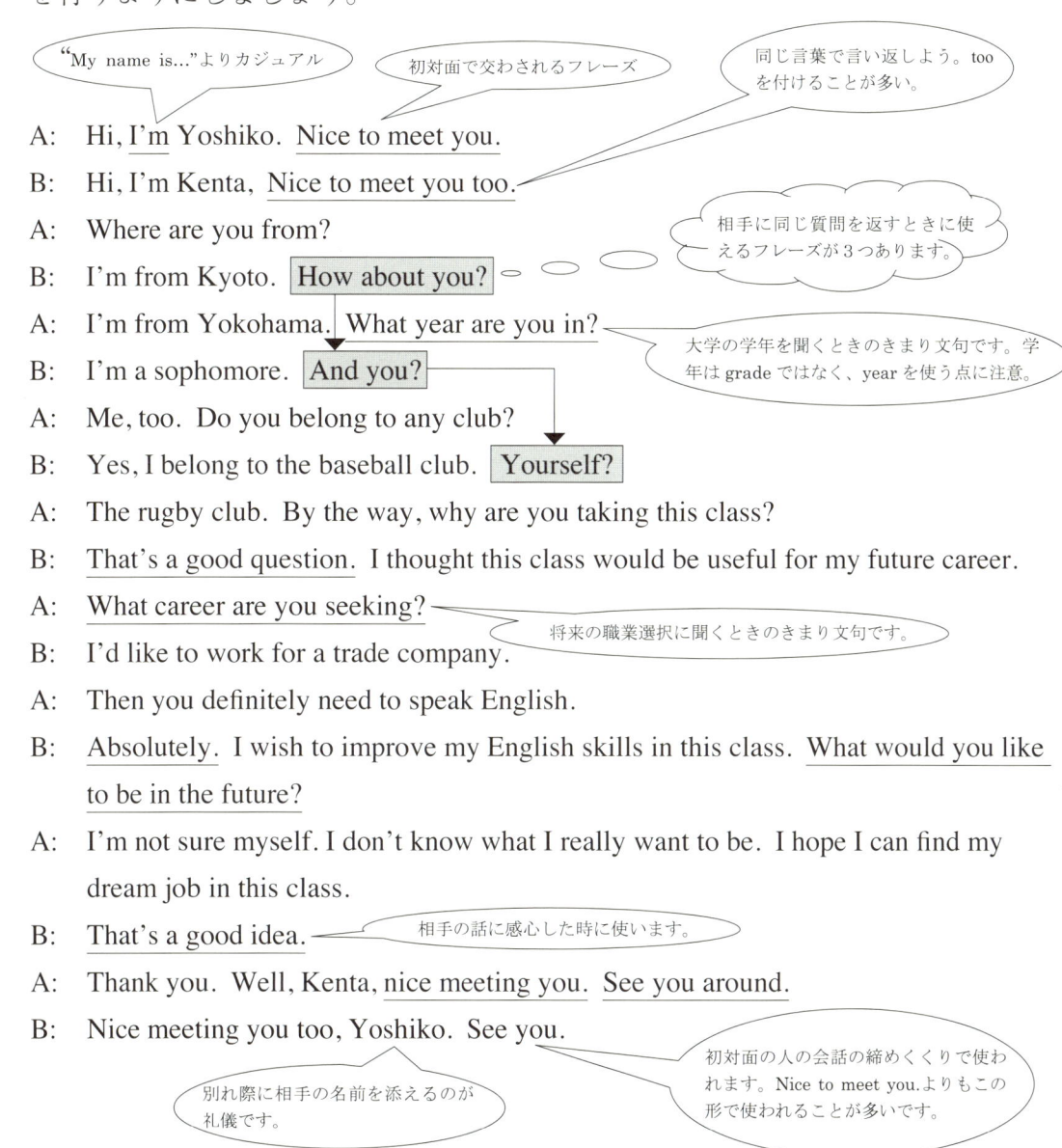

A: Hi, I'm Yoshiko. Nice to meet you. （"My name is..."よりカジュアル／初対面で交わされるフレーズ）

B: Hi, I'm Kenta. Nice to meet you too. （同じ言葉で言い返そう。too を付けることが多い。）

A: Where are you from?

B: I'm from Kyoto. How about you? （相手に同じ質問を返すときに使えるフレーズが３つあります。）

A: I'm from Yokohama. What year are you in? （大学の学年を聞くときのきまり文句です。学年は grade ではなく、year を使う点に注意。）

B: I'm a sophomore. And you?

A: Me, too. Do you belong to any club?

B: Yes, I belong to the baseball club. Yourself?

A: The rugby club. By the way, why are you taking this class?

B: That's a good question. I thought this class would be useful for my future career.

A: What career are you seeking? （将来の職業選択に聞くときのきまり文句です。）

B: I'd like to work for a trade company.

A: Then you definitely need to speak English.

B: Absolutely. I wish to improve my English skills in this class. What would you like to be in the future?

A: I'm not sure myself. I don't know what I really want to be. I hope I can find my dream job in this class.

B: That's a good idea. （相手の話に感心した時に使います。）

A: Thank you. Well, Kenta, nice meeting you. See you around.

B: Nice meeting you too, Yoshiko. See you.

（別れ際に相手の名前を添えるのが礼儀です。）

（初対面の人の会話の締めくくりで使われます。Nice to meet you. よりもこの形で使われることが多いです。）

135

Appendix 2
Useful Dialogs for Business Persons

初対面

A:	Nice to meet you.	A:	はじめまして。
B:	Nice to meet you, too.	B:	はじめまして。

A:	It's a great pleasure to meet you.	A:	お会いできてうれしいです。
B:	The pleasure is mine.	B:	こちらこそ。

A:	I'm pleased to meet you.	A:	お会いできてうれしいです。
B:	I'm pleased to meet you, too.	B:	こちらこそ。

A:	I'm glad to see you.	A:	お会いできてうれしいです。
B:	I'm glad to see you too.	B:	こちらこそ。

A:	How do you do?	A:	お初にお目にかかります。
B:	How do you do?	B:	お初にお目にかかります。

A:	Are you by chance Mr. Yamamoto?	A:	もしかして山本さんですか。
B:	Yes. Have we met?	B:	そうですが、お会いしたことがありましたか。

More Vocabulary
Do you know me? / Do I know you?

A:	You must be Ms. Yamamoto.	A:	山本さんですよね。
B:	Yes.	B:	そうですが。

A:	Is this your first time here?	A:	当地は初めてですか。
B:	No, this is my second time.	B:	いいえ、二回目です。

Appendix

A:	How did you get here?	A:	こちらへはどのようにいらっしゃいましたか。
B:	I got [came] here by taxi.	B:	タクシーで参りました。

More Vocabulary

by car / by limousine / by bus / by train / by trolley / by streetcar / by tram / by subway / by bicycle / by motorcycle / by bike / by moped / by boat / by ship / by submarine / by plane / by airplane / by helicopter / by ambulance / by ropeway / by rickshaw / by walking / on foot

A:	How long are you going to stay here?	A:	当地にはどのくらい滞在される予定ですか。
B:	Just a couple of days.	B:	二、三日です。

More Vocabulary

A few days. / Several days.

プロフィールを聞く

A:	What's your name?	A:	お名前は？
B:	My name is Michael Kaneko. You can call me Michael.	B:	マイケル・金子と申します。マイケルとお呼びいただければ。

More Vocabulary

Call me Michael. / People call me Michael. / Some people call me Michael. / My nickname is Michael.

A:	May I have your name, please?	A:	お名前をお伺いしてもよろしいでしょうか。
B:	Sure, my name is Wakura Yoshiko.	B:	はい、和倉よしこと申します。

A:	What did you say your name was?	A:	お名前は何とおっしゃいましたか。
B:	My name is HOSOKI Kenta.	B:	細木健太です。

More Vocabulary

May I have your name again, please? / Your name again?

A:	Where are you from?	A:	どちらからいらっしゃいましたか。
B:	I'm from Sapporo.	B:	札幌から参りました。

More Vocabulary
Where do [did] you come from?

A:	Are you from here?	A:	地元の方ですか。
B:	Yes.	B:	はい。

More Vocabulary
Are you local? (= Are you from here?) / Do you live here?

職業、勤務先、職務

A:	What do you do for a living?	A:	ご職業は何ですか。
B:	I run a restaurant.	B:	レストランを経営しています。

More Vocabulary
run a restaurant [coffee shop / flower shop / barber shop / bar / store / chain of convenience store / supermarket / grocery store / liquor store / cram school / kindergarten / nursery school / elementary school / high school / college / junior college / university / vocational school / hospital / clinic / dentist office / farm / gas station / souvenir shop / parking lot / repair shop / bath house /

A:	What is your occupation [job / profession]?	A:	どちらにお務めですか。
B:	I work for the government.	B:	公務員です。

A:	Who do you work for?	A:	どちらにお務めですか。
B:	I work for a trade company.	B:	貿易会社（商社）に勤務しています。

A:	What kind of business do you run?	A:	どんな会社を経営されていますか。
B:	I run an Italian restaurant.	B:	イタリアレストランを経営しています。

More Vocabulary
What sort of [type of] business do you run?

A:	Who do you work for?	A:	どちらにお務めですか。
B:	I am a civil servant [public servant / government worker].	B:	公務員です。

More Vocabulary
municipal government employee（地方公務員）/ local government employee（地方公務員）/ national government employee（国家公務員）/ police officer（警察官）/ judge（裁判官、判事）/ prosecutor（検察官、検事）/ firefighter（消防士）/ paramedic（救命士）/ Self-Defense Force officer（自衛官）/ Coast Guard officer（海上保安官）/ member of the House of Representatives（衆議院議員）/ member of the House of Councilors（参議院議員）/ member of a (the) local assembly（地方議会議員）/ member of a (the) prefectural [ward / city / town / village] assembly（県議会議員［区議会議員、市議会議員、町議会議員、村議会議員］）

A:	Where do you work?	A:	勤務地はどちらですか。
B:	I work in Tokyo.	B:	東京です。

A:	In which section do you work?	A:	どの部署で働いていますか。
B:	I work in the personnel department [section].	B:	人事部(課)に所属しています。

More Vocabulary
public relations section（広報課）/ finance section（財務課）/ sales department（販売部）

A:	What are your duties in your company?	A:	会社ではどんな仕事をされていますか。
B:	I am the secretary to the president.	B:	社長秘書をしております。

More Vocabulary
chauffeur（お抱え運転手）/ security guard（ガードマン）/ parking lot worker（駐車場係）/ janitor（清掃係）/ boilerman（ボイラー係）/ telephone operator（電話交換手）

A:	What are your duties in your company?	A:	会社ではどんな仕事をされていますか。
B:	I'm in charge of public relations.	B:	広報を担当しております。

A: What is your position in your company?
B: I am the president.

A: 職位は何ですか。
B: 社長です。

More Vocabulary
vice president（副社長）/ representative director （代表取締役）/ executive [senior] managing director（専務取締役）/ managing director（常務取締役）/ chairman; chairwoman; chairperson（会長）/ adviser（顧問）/ CEO (Chief Executive Officer)（最高経営責任者）/ COO (Chief Operating Officer)（最高執行責任者）/ CFO (Chief Financial Officer)（最高財務責任者）/ branch manager（支店長）/ department manager（部長）/ section manager（課長）/ subsection manager; chief clerk（係長）/ chief（主任）/ vice chief（次長）

Appendix 3
Describing OUC

STEP 1: Describing Your University

　国際ビジネスマンには自社の概要や業務内容を英語で語るスキルが求められます。ここでは、まず皆さんの母校である商大の概要を英語でできるように練習しましょう。大学のサイトを参考に、以下の和文の大学概要をまず完成させて、対応する英訳文の空欄に適切な語句を書き入れてください。

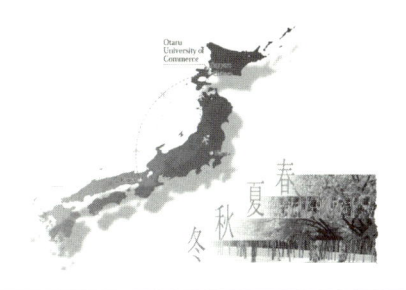

1 大学名	:_____
2 創立年	:_____
3 所在地	:_____
4 郵便番号	:_____
5 学　長	:_____
6 学　部	:_____
7 学生数	:_____

1 University Name	:_____
2 Founded	:_____
3 Address	:_____
4 _____	:_____
5 _____	:_____
6 Undergraduate program	:_____
7 Number of Students	:_____

STEP 2: Being Interviewed about Your University

　商大のことをあまりよく知らない人から、大学について矢継ぎ早に英語で質問を受けている状況を想定してください。前のStepで習った商大に関する知識を使って、空欄に正確な情報を入れながら対話文をペアで読んでください。一度終わったら、立場を交代して行ってください。

A: Hi, I'm _____. Nice to meet you.

B: Hi, I'm _____. Nice to meet you too.

A: Where do you go to school?

B: I go to _____.

A: Oh, do you? Could you tell me something about your university?

B: Sure. What would you like to know?

A: What kind of university is it?

B: It is a _____ university for those wishing to learn _____.

A: Where is it located?

B: It is located_____.

A: What is the size of the campus?

B: The campus is _____ with _____ square meters.

A: How many students are enrolled?

B: About _____ students are enrolled.

A: When was it founded?

B: It was founded in _____.

A: What kinds of faculties and departments do you have?

B: It has the faculty of _____.

A: What is your university famous for?

B: It is famous for _____.

A: What do you like and dislike about your university?

B: I like the _____ of the university but do not like the _____.

Appendix 4
交通機関の標識 (A)

アメリカの街中で見られる標識を見て、設問に答えてください。

SIGNS IN AMERICA

	画像	英文	設問と選択肢
1		SILENCE AND RESPECT	ここはどこ？ A: 教会 B: 墓地 C: 火葬場
2		SIDEWALK CLOSED USE OTHER SIDE	下線部の意味は？ A: 歩道 B: 順路 C: 通路
3		If there is too much noise, report it to the circulation desk.	下線部の意味は？ A: 閲覧 B: 貸出 C: 返却
4		get your prescriptions filled while you shop.	下線部の意味は？ A: 診断書 B: 処方箋 C: 同意書

143

5		Can't Decide On A Gift? <u>Gift Certificates</u> Available in Any Amount	下線部の意味は？ A: 商品券 B: 割引券 C: 引換券
6		<u>NO LOITERING</u> IN A POSTED NO TRANSPASSING AREA	下線部の意味は？ A: うろつき B: 座り込み C: 寝そべり
7		PLEASE PARDON OUR <u>DUST</u>.	下線部の意味は？ A: 粉 B: 塵 C: 埃
8		<u>TOW AWAY</u> NO STOPPING ANY TIME	下線部の意味は？ A: 移動 B: 収納 C: 解体
9		AT THE FIRST <u>REGISTER</u>	下線部の意味は？ A: 予約 B: 入館 C: 退室
10		NO <u>TRESPASSING</u> AT OTHER TIMES	下線部の意味は？ A: 立ち入り B: 横断 C: 退去

Appendix 5
交通機関の標識 (B)

イギリスの街中で見られる標識を見て、設問に答えてください。

	画像	英文	設問と選択肢
1		Danger <u>Demolition in Progress</u>	下線部の意味は？ A: 建設中 B: 修理中 C: 解体中
2		Face <u>direction of travel</u>	下線部の意味は？ A: 旅先 B: 進行方向 C: 形跡
3		Automatic smoke door: <u>Keep clear</u>	下線部の意味は？ A: 清潔に B: 物を置くな C: 近づくな
4		PLEASE WAIT HERE UNTIL <u>CALLED</u>	下線部の意味は？ A: 電話を受ける B: 名前を呼ばれる C: 注意される

5		FOOTPATH CLOSED	下線部の意味は？ 　A: 歩道 　B: 回廊 　C: 地下道
6		MIND THE GAP	注意書きの意味は？ 　A: 段差に注意 　B: 隙間に注意 　C: 滑りに注意
7		Unsuitable for Long Vehicle	下線部の意味は？ 　A: 車高が高い車両 　B: 縦長の車両 　C: 幅のある車両
8		Humps for 50 yards	下線部の意味は？ 　A: マンホール 　B: コブ 　C: 凹み
9		Diverted Traffic	注意書きの意味は？ 　A: 迂回せよ 　B: 引き返せ 　C: 近寄るな
10		GIVE WAY	注意書きの意味は？ 　A: 道を進め 　B: 道を譲れ 　C: 道を引き返せ